Inside the Not So HALLOWED HALLS

A Funny Thing Happened at School Today

Dewitt Jones, Ed.D.

Library of Congress Control Number: 2004096721
ISBN: 0-9760572-0-4

Edited, Designed, and Manufactured by

FRP™

P.O. Box 305142
Nashville, Tennessee 37230
800-358-0560

Story Editor: Randy McDonald
Project Editor: Nicki Pendleton Wood
Art Director: Steve Newman
Book design: Bill Kersey
Cover design: Jeremy Jones
Cover image, © Creatas Stock Resources

Manufactured in the United States of America
First printing: 2005
5,000 copies

For additional copies, please visit www.realschoolstories.com.

Dedication

Inside the Not So Hallowed Halls is dedicated to my great aunt, Florence Jarvis. Florence taught kindergarten in the Des Moines Independent School District for over forty years. She would look at me with her special smile and say, "You can do anything you want in life, but you must try hard and always be honest." She was a very special person and touched so many people.

Special thanks:

Jeremy Jones, Graphic Designer
Jeremy Jones is a graphic designer in Des Moines, Iowa. Jeremy, my youngest son, actually came up with the title for this book and designed the cover.

Shawn Bauer, Project Assistant
Shawn Bauer, my project assistant responsible for editing, managing speaking engagements, public relations, and marketing, lives in Mayville, Wisconsin, with her husband and two daughters.

Introduction

*W*hen I started my first principal assignment in the fall of 1973, a veteran teacher came into my office and said, "I am retiring at the end of this school year and if I had it to do all over again, I would keep a journal of those things that happened that were sad, silly, or unusual. I've forgotten many of them now but if I had taken time to write them down during my thirty-five–year career, I could write a great book. My advice to you is don't wait—start now!"

From that day forward, at the age of twenty-seven, I have entered into my daily planner notes from over 400 situations, some humorous, others heartbreaking. With the intention of writing this book, I have stored my planners in boxes and moved those boxes from new home to new home as my career opportunities expanded.

This first volume of *Inside the Not So Hallowed Halls* contains real-life stories about happenings in public school settings that I have experienced in my roles as a teacher, middle school principal, high school principal, and superintendent of schools in three school systems in two states. Some of the stories are funny, some are sad, and some contain lessons learned which will hopefully benefit those interested in entering the education profession.

Since we have all had school experiences, the stories may resurrect a memory or emotion from something that occurred in the readers' school lives that may have been similar—a hook into their past or present. Each story takes the reader into and through the situation and, I hope, allows the reader to experience the emotions of the participants and remember their own school friends, teachers, principals, peers, or fellow staff members. *Inside the Not So Hallowed Halls* provides an opportunity for readers associated with education to daydream about their past or present school experiences and to reminisce and share with friends how these stories or characters relate to their lives.

Disclaimer

Inside the Not So Hallowed Halls includes stories based on actual occurrences. All names have been changed. In many cases, grade levels, subject matter, and class assignments have also been changed. Since all the names are fictitious, any similarities to people with the same name are coincidental.

TABLE OF CONTENTS

WHAT ARE WE HERE FOR?

Out of the mouths of babes. . .

On a brisk but sunny morning in October, Mr. Dawson, an elementary school principal, arrived for work at 7:20 a.m. and noticed a young boy alone on a swing across the playground. It was unusual for a student to arrive that early. Mr. Dawson paused at the steps and decided to check on the boy to make sure everything was all right. As he walked across the yard, he saw that it was Eli, a second grade student.

Mr. Dawson knew that Eli came every morning for the breakfast program being provided at the school for kids who otherwise might not get breakfast. Still, it was awfully early for Eli to be there, since the breakfast wasn't served until 8:00 a.m.

Eli waved and smiled as Mr. Dawson reached the swings. "Eli, how are you this morning?"

"Just fine, Mr. Dawson," Eli replied, continuing to swing. "How about you?"

"Fine, just fine," Mr. Dawson smiled back. He still wasn't sure, though, why Eli was at school so early. He hoped everything was all right in Eli's home life, but, not wanting to probe too directly, Mr. Dawson prompted, "Are you here for the breakfast program?"

Eli stopped his swing, looked up to the bright, clear October sky, thought for a moment, then said to Mr. Dawson in a very serious second grade manner, "Nope, I'm here for the whole thing."

Mr. Dawson went to work that day marveling at the ways in which wisdom finds us.

When he shared this story with me as his superintendent some time later, we certainly laughed, but we also realized the power of Eli's comment as a pointed focus for the roles of teachers and school administrators.

As educational leaders, are we as wise as little Eli? Are we here for "the whole thing?" Are we here for the kids who struggle with learning? Are we here for the kids who come from poorer homes? For those who don't speak English as their first language? For minority children? For those with special needs? For those who are gifted and talented?

To this day, Eli's comment has stayed with me. I have passed on his wisdom in keynote addresses and speeches I've given to faculty and staff, always to a warm reception. A little boy taught me a big lesson, maybe even a universal lesson. But certainly in the field of education, we all must greet each day fully prepared to be there for "the whole thing."

Note from a high school parent:

I know this will be an unexcused absence, but Larry likes to hunt and for the last three days he has been pheasant hunting with his friends. I know his friends' parents will tell the school they were sick or something, but I just can't lie to you about this. Larry is not happy that I won't say he was sick like his friends, but we have argued about it enough. Do what you have to—he was hunting with his friends. Can he make up his schoolwork?

THE GREAT SPIDER PANIC OF 1978

It crawls the walls and halls—or does it?

On my desk sits a somewhat somber souvenir. It is a large, hairy tarantula, its sinister clusters of eyes staring back at any gaze, fangs peeking menacingly below; the thing is frozen in mid-crawl, encased in a glass paperweight. It might cause a visitor to cast a surreptitious sideways glance at me and wonder how and why this curiosity came to occupy a place of honor among the effects of a former principal—as you also might wonder and with good reason.

It began on a Wednesday school morning much like any other. As principal, I was standing in the hallway greeting kids and visiting with faculty as they arrived. I was surprised, then, when I happened to glance down a hall and see the sixth grade science teacher, Alice Marshall, striding purposefully toward me, her face a mask of worry or concern or *something* certainly not the usual.

Mrs. Marshall was an excellent educator, previously named middle level science teacher of the year. She kept an eclectic collection of animals in her classroom for the students to study and observe, both vertebrates and invertebrates, stuffed and alive. Students in her six daily classes had before-school responsibilities each week for feeding, cleaning, and taking care of the live animals, birds, and spiders. The students loved coming in early to help Mrs. Marshall with these chores, and parents who drove their kids to school would even drop in and offer a helping hand.

It was doubly odd, then, to see her at this hour not in her classroom tending the animals but approaching me with some urgency. She came up to me and quietly said she needed to see me in the office right away. We stepped out of the morning hustle and bustle into the relative quiet of my office so I could hear the news.

A tarantula had escaped.

Two of the favorite attractions in Mrs. Marshall's classroom had always been the two glass cages that each housed a very impressive tarantula. The tops of the cages were made of perforated metal that was heavy so the spider could not push its way out. When students cleaned these cages, they wore heavy padded gloves to protect from bites, and Mrs. Marshall was always on hand to supervise.

Next to those cages there was a large yellow information card with basic facts: "Tarantulas are members of the spider family *Theraphosidae* (order *Araneae*). Our tarantulas are brown and their body length is about two inches long. Their legs are about two to three inches long and they have kind of a bald spot on their hairy backs. They have eight eyes grouped very closely together, large fangs, and while their bite would hurt, the harm to humans is nonexistent." The spiders, however ominous they might appear, were not really any threat to humans.

On this particular Wednesday morning, as the students approached the cages for their chores, they noticed something odd: the perforated metal top of one of the tarantula cages was slid back, sideways, across the top. They looked in carefully. The spider was gone.

At first there had been a general search around the room, but when no sign of the beast turned up, Mrs. Marshall asked the students to leave the classroom so she could lock up. She explained that tarantulas move pretty fast, that it could have escaped the room already, and she needed to report the missing eight-legged menace to the office—since school was going to start in approximately 15 minutes!

And now here she was with me. And while both Mrs. Marshall and I knew the spider wasn't a real threat to anyone, we also knew what kind of effect a loose tarantula crawling through the halls might have!

In ten minutes, students would be entering the science wing. I could just imagine the announcement over the intercom, "Students and faculty, please be on the lookout for a tarantula which we think is on the loose in the science wing. But don't worry—its bite is the only thing that will hurt you!" We simply would have to find the spider before we could open that wing for students. I asked Mrs. Marshall to have her student helpers leave that area while I went to look for the custodian and recruited other volunteers to help search.

In the teacher's lounge I explained the situation to about ten teachers who seemed to find the predicament awfully funny—until I said I needed volunteers to help in the hunt. Only three agreed to help, the rest not willing to risk getting bitten by what surely now would be a frightened and disoriented spider.

Then the first bell sounded, signaling to students that they could enter the academic wings and go into the classrooms. I quickly posted a teacher at the entrance to the science wing to stop students, then went on to head the hunt.

Naturally, the sentry-teacher posted guarding the science wing was grilled by curious middle school students and eventually relented, telling students that a tarantula from the sixth grade science room had escaped and was on the prowl somewhere in the school.

That was all it took. There was laughter, sure, but some of it was very nervous laughter, and it soon mixed in with growing panic in the hallway. Instinctively, students looked down to the floor hoping not to see the spider, then to the walls, the ceilings, the air ducts. Then the rumor mill started. In less than five minutes, 500 kids were asking their teachers whether they might die if bitten by the spider. Some even wanted to call their parents to go home.

While we searched the science wing, I learned that word was spreading like wildfire around the school, so I asked Mrs. Marshall to get on the intercom as quickly as she could and remind the kids that tarantulas are harmless, to tell them that it would be found shortly, and not to worry. She did an admirable job—and then I heard her finish with, "If you see it, do not try to pick it up as it might get frightened and bite you! Please just let your teacher know and someone will come and get it!"

Well, bless her heart for trying, but that really didn't help. In fact, it made the situation worse. It wasn't complete pandemonium, but the buzz among the students in the halls swelled, and now some kids were absolutely imploring teachers to let them call home. Even some teachers were becoming uncomfortable.

After five seemingly endless minutes, the art teacher found the tarantula in the school's media center behind a book that was on display on a top shelf, to my immeasurable relief. Mrs. Marshall put on her gloves, caught the spider, and returned it to its cage. She then announced over the intercom that the Great Spider Panic was over and done: the tarantula had been found and was safely in its cage.

Things calmed down and classes returned to normal, or at least as normal as middle school classes are after some excitement that breaks the daily routines. For me, alas, the drama did not end with the return of the tarantula to its own routine life.

The next day, the phones in the school office rang and rang with angry parents calling to find out how this could have happened and demanding to know why these terrible spiders were allowed in our science room. Some wanted to know what we were going to do to the obviously "irresponsible teacher." Most of their concerns were put to rest when we read them the information about the tarantula, and by then we had finally solved the mystery of how the tarantula had managed to escape. The evening custodian, who liked to watch the tarantulas, had moved the perforated metal lid aside on one of the cages so he could give the spider a little push to watch it move around the cage. Returning to his duties, he just forgot to replace the lid to its original closed position, for which he was very sorry. So at length, the parents who had reacted strongly to the incident were brought to understanding.

But then the newspaper ran the story! They did a fairly good job of reporting the entire incident, and, while the article was fine, the headline was as sensationalized as they could have made it: "Poisonous Spider on the Loose in Local Middle School."

In responsible response, the sixth grade students themselves wrote a very good report on the incident, that the paper, to its credit, printed. It was much more educational than the newspaper's version, and it helped to put the public's lingering concerns to rest. But this story was the talk of the town for quite a while!

At the next parent/teacher conferences, I think there was 100% attendance by parents of sixth grade students. Mrs. Marshall noted with a wry smile and reported to me that they all read the card next to the cage and looked at the tarantulas as they entered or left the room.

So how did I come by this frightful remembrance of the Great Spider Panic that decorates my desk?

When the tarantula died a few years later, Mrs. Marshall had it made into a clear glass paperweight for me so I would never forget the experience—as if I could! Each time I look at it, I laugh, recalling how much excitement was packed into those twenty minutes on that out-of-the-ordinary Wednesday morning.

Call from an upset parent about school letting out early:

"Who makes the decision to let school out early? This is ridiculous. When I was in school we never called off school for anything. I have a job and don't have time for this." When the secretary told the parent that the superintendent made the final decision she said, "Tell him that he can watch my kids until I get off work since he has so much time on his hands."

BIRTHDAY SURPRISE, BIRTHDAY SCANDAL

"What do we do with these, teacher?"

In many schools, children celebrate their birthdays by bringing treats from home and proudly distributing them to their classmates. This elementary school ritual certainly is innocent enough, but one hapless grade school teacher found out just how wrong it can go when "birthday surprise" became "birthday scandal."

Mrs. Miller was fantastic. She was the state's runner-up teacher of the year and was the most requested teacher in the school where she taught, which was part of the school system where I was superintendent at the time. She was *very* conscientious about the responsibility of being entrusted with the growth and shaping of young and inquisitive minds. Her second grade classroom was always a busy, living demonstration of an outstanding creative learning environment. Mrs. Miller's room was proudly showcased to visitors for her innovative bulletin boards and the ingenious ways she matched her classroom themes to the lessons her students were studying.

Sally was a sweet girl in Mrs. Miller's class and a very good student whose birthday had come around on a pleasant Thursday. Crisply dressed for the occasion, Sally arrived at school that morning and daintily handed Mrs. Miller the unassuming paper sack of treats she had brought for the class to share. Mrs. Miller said that Sally could pass them out near the end of the day.

So about fifteen minutes before the end of the school day, Mrs. Miller announced to the second graders that there was a birthday girl in the room, and the whole class sang *Happy Birthday* to a beaming Sally. Mrs. Miller then handed Sally the small paper sack Sally had brought containing the treats for the class. Proudly, Sally reached in and handed the first one to Mrs. Miller. With her attention fully on thanking Sally very much, Mrs. Miller idly placed the treat on her desk, a cursory glance telling her that it was a chocolate "coin" wrapped in gold foil. She knew these to be a favorite candy with kids.

As Sally went off around the classroom distributing the treats, Mrs. Miller turned to erase the blackboard. She had just put down the eraser and picked up chalk to write the year of Sally's birth on the board when Mrs. Miller heard the most curious snapping sounds behind her in the midst of the normal hubbub of a birthday break.

She turned to locate the source of the snapping and found a classroom full of active, curious second graders who were waving, stretching, snapping, and attempting to blow up long translucent balloons. Mrs. Miller's heart did not achieve a full stop, but came close. The chalk hit the floor.

The "treats" were condoms.

Mrs. Miller and her heart recovered quickly out of sheer necessity, and she calmly began to gather up the collection from the first row of perplexed faces, telling the children they were a different kind of balloon than Sally had expected and needed to be returned. Then she called the principal's office.

It wasn't long at all before the phone was ringing in my office. The superintendent usually hears quickly from school principals about things that are potentially serious so that school board members can be notified. No board member appreciates surprises on the evening news.

Mrs. Miller's principal somehow managed to keep it businesslike while relating to me what happened. When he had finished, neither of us could suppress laughter, though we knew the incident could have difficult repercussions. He was sure that Mrs. Miller had the situation under control. Each parent would be called immediately, told what had taken place, and assured that the kids were not aware of what they had been given. It then fell to me to call the school board members.

Back in the classroom, Mrs. Miller consoled Sally, who thought for all the world that she was bringing chocolate coins for her classmates. She explained that she had forgotten to tell her mom in time that she wanted to bring treats to school on her birthday, so that morning she had gone into her dad's top dresser drawer where she knew he kept "chocolate coins." She dutifully had counted out twenty-three and put them in the paper sack to take to school. She didn't know they were balloons!

The most difficult call Mrs. Miller had to make was to Sally's parents to tell them what had happened. Mrs. Miller was hoping that Sally's father would not answer the phone. But of course, he did. Taking a deep breath, Mrs. Miller explained what had happened. The chagrined man apologized profusely and offered to do anything he could to make things right with the other parents. Mrs. Miller assured him she could explain it to the parents adequately.

By 5:30 p.m. that day all the parents had been contacted. With the exception of one parent who just didn't understand how this could have happened, everything went fine. The press never got wind of the story, which would have made certain headlines. The school board, naturally, wanted to make sure that teachers "more closely monitor treats in the future," meaning, I guess, that they wanted more protection in place.

Mrs. Miller, still in awed disbelief at the nearly impossible series of events, later told the story of her *faux pas* to the district's improvement team. Everyone laughed good naturedly, and all were so glad it hadn't happened to them. Of course everyone teased her about it for the rest of the year, about which she forever was a good sport.

The incident didn't hamper Mrs. Miller professionally—on the contrary, her graceful, reassuring handling of the situation and clear concern for children are qualities very much in demand for an administrator. Mrs. Miller is currently an excellent elementary school principal.

As for Sally, I don't know whether she'll someday remember the events of her second grade birthday celebration and the curious balloons, finally realizing what they were. If she does I sincerely hope it will bring her a delighted laugh.

THE SNARER SNARED

Smoking Wars Part I: A teacher gets caught in a trap of her own.

There must be an axiom that exists somewhere along the lines of "any prohibition begets rebellion against it," and the prohibition against smoking in school has made for a cops-and-robbers game between faculty and students that has gone on for decades. Nobody ever really wins The Smoking Wars, but the battle goes on unabated. Rarely, though, does it achieve the level of slapstick comedy that it did one unforgettable Monday morning.

A seventh grader named Sue was an inveterate and ingenious smoker. She was an elusive smoker, the Gray Ghost of smoking, because though the faculty all knew that she was smoking at every opportunity, no one could catch her at it. She was cunning. She was careful. She was cagey.

Sue became the topic of way too many conversations in the counseling office and the principal's office. This outlaw's name even made it into a monthly faculty meeting where, of course, the topic was, "How do we get Sue to stop smoking in the girl's restroom?" No matter how hard anyone tried to catch her, she outfoxed all.

When the next year began, with Sue going into the eighth grade, one of the teachers, Linda, finally made Sue's smoking a personal crusade. With jaw set, she absolutely determined to orchestrate some plan to lay a snare for Smoking Sue, get the goods on her, and march her to the office for long-overdue just rewards. Linda probably should have watched more Road Runner cartoons before crafting her plans, but she was not to be dissuaded.

Finally Linda had her strategy.

Enough anecdotal reports of Sue's habits in the girl's restroom had been collected that Linda knew Sue carefully looked under all the stalls to make sure they were empty before locking herself in one and lighting up. This, Linda believed, was Sue's Achilles heel. And though a heel would loom large in the ensuing legend, it wasn't Sue's.

At 10:00 a.m. on the fateful Monday morning, Linda entered the girl's restroom, went into the stall next to where it was believed Sue usually smoked, took off her shoes, crossed her legs, and sat silently on the stool.

It wasn't long before someone entered the restroom, and Linda's heartbeat picked up. Sure enough, whoever it was went from stall to stall and stopped, peering under the doors. In a moment the door to the stall next to Linda's was opened, closed, and locked. There was silence.

Then came the sound of a striking match, followed by the acrid smell of match sulphur and cigarette smoke. The moment was at hand! This was it! Slowly and quietly Linda began to uncross her legs and stand up on the stool to peer over and catch Sue in the act. She had one bare foot firmly on the toilet seat, the other coming to meet it, hands steadied against the stall walls. She pushed up suddenly with her foot to raise herself all the way in one quick "gotcha!" motion—and her foot slipped off the toilet seat!

SPLASH! Into the toilet her foot went at a frightening velocity, so fast, with such force, that it wedged into the narrow opening at the bottom! In almost the same instant Linda heard the final insult: the hissssss and flush of a hastily extinguished cigarette in the next stall, which banged open, as footsteps beat a hasty exit from the restroom.

Cursing under her breath, Linda jerked at her foot to give chase—and discovered that she was stuck fast.

Her foot was so tightly wedged in the bottom of the toilet that no matter how hard she wiggled and pulled, she could not get her foot out of the toilet! Brer Rabbit and the Tar Baby had nothing on her! Her foot literally was "caught in a trap."

Now panic started to set in. Finally Linda heard another girl come into the restroom, and she called out, sending the startled and befuddled girl to the office for help.

Help came running and did all they could not to laugh—well, not too hard, anyway, and only outside. The custodian, the principal, an industrial arts teacher, and a math teacher, all came to help release Linda's foot, but to no avail. No matter how much everyone tried, no one could get the exasperated teacher's foot unstuck from the bottom of the toilet.

Finally, a physical education teacher who also happened to be a volunteer paramedic was called as a last resort before calling for real emergency crews. His combination of muscles and skills finally worked to extract Linda's swollen foot from the porcelain trap. Linda had an epiphany that she perhaps was better suited for teaching than detective work.

And the wily Sue escaped unscathed to torment teachers and smoke another day.

MYNAH BIRD BLUE STREAK

Parents get an earful.

One of the oddest situations I encountered as a middle school principal was when one of my sixth grade science teachers, Ann, announced that she had acquired a rare bird. Ann loved animals and she already had many of them, both stuffed and alive, in her classroom. She thought that the Indian mynah bird, a member of the grackle family, would be a fun addition to her collection. The mynah bird, of course, can be taught to mimic words and phrases in an adult-like voice, along with many other sounds and even some songs. Ann knew this would be fun for her students.

School had been in session for two weeks when the mynah bird joined our middle school "family." It was a beautiful animal, with velvet black feathers, a white spot on each wing, and a bright yellow beak. It wasn't very large, only about ten to twelve inches long, so it easily fit into a cage in the classroom. While this bird didn't "talk" yet, it knew how to make a loud screech when startled or wanting to get our attention. To quiet the bird, Ann would cover its cage with a cloth.

Ann's students loved the live creatures in the room, especially the new bird. Each class section took turns coming to school early in the morning before school to clean cages and feed the animals. In addition to their regular chores, Ann gave the students sets of words to start teaching the mynah bird. To their delight, during the course of the next month the bird started to mimic certain words such as "Hello." As you can imagine, Ann was beamingly proud of her new bird.

That changed in October.

The students were working during third period one fine fall day while Ann was going about her normal teaching routine, when all of a sudden, in a very loud, shrieking voice, the bird said, "shiiiiiit!"

The ensuing silence was deafening—though not for long. The students burst out into gales of laughter. Ann did not. She immediately covered the bird's cage so it would stop talking. Alarmed, she came to my office after class to report that the bird had started swearing. Well, unless we had a zoological miracle on our hands, birds don't natively start using human swear words, so it was clear that someone had taught the bird this word. She was determined to find out who.

The next morning Ann arrived in my office with three sixth grade boys in tow who sheepishly admitted to teaching the bird to say "shit." We learned that they also had added "damn it" to its repertoire. Yes, they knew it was wrong; they just thought it would be fun to see if they could actually teach the bird to say some bad words.

With, I admit, some extraordinary effort, I managed to put on my serious "principal face," and I instructed the boys in no uncertain terms to discontinue their "training." I asked Ann to call each of their parents.

That seemed to be the end of the mynah bird issues. That changed in November.

The bird spontaneously just started to say "shiiiiiit" very loudly and then follow it up with "damn it" equally loudly. He also interjected pleasantries, such as "hello" and "sit down" into his blue streaks. He said these words so loudly that he could be heard in the hallway outside the science pod. When this started, Ann would cover the cage. Sometimes he quit; sometimes he went right on lecturing. The laughter in the course room would get uncontrollable.

That was bad enough, but this was the week of the November parent/teacher conferences, and the place soon would be thick with parents. Ann promised that she would put the bird back in the science storeroom and cover the cage. It was quiet and dark in that area, which usually kept the bird quiet, and it was more distant from the main areas where the parents would be visiting the school. That seemed to me to be a good way to deal with it.

That changed on the day of the conferences.

Conferences began at noon and everything was going along smoothly until about 5:30 p.m. I was walking down the hallway leading to the science pod, smiling, nodding, shaking hands, greeting parents headed to their next conference, when all of a sudden, a high-pitched, shrieking voice yelled "shiiiiit!"

All motion stopped.

"What was that?" parents were asking each other. Before I could even open my mouth to answer, the same shrieking voice yelled, "Damn it!"

I excused myself and hurried to the science area where parents were waiting for their conferences. Most of them were curious about what the noise could be, except for the parents gathered in front of the sixth grade classroom. They already knew because their kids had told them all about the mynah bird.

Ann came out of the science storage room managing somehow to look red-faced and pale at the same time and began apologizing for the bird's behavior. Even though she had covered the cage, the bird continued to shriek "shiiiiit" at the top of its lungs.

I was beginning to wonder what mynah bird stew might taste like as a small crowd began to gather in the science pod curious to know what the noise was all about. Ann said she was going to take the bird home.

Duty calling as loudly as that accursed cursing bird, I explained the situation carefully to the parents, most of whom thought it was pretty funny. Predictably there were a few who were very upset that their kids had been exposed to such language at school. (I so wished the bird had screeched about then, "Sit down, damn it!")

Ann decided to keep the mynah bird at home as a pet and not bring it back to school, but old Dirty Bird was memorialized in photo in the Middle School Yearbook for all to remember.

Note from a sixth grade parent:

Please excuse Sally from school yesterday. She had her first .

NOW HEAR THIS!

P.A. system follies.

Anyone who has never heard an announcement read over the loud speaker in school, raise their hand. Anybody? Anybody?

Sometimes students did the reading in our schools and other times a secretary or the principal would read them. In my first high school principalship, it was customary for the principal to read the daily announcements in the morning, with the secretary making any special announcements throughout the school day.

By the end of my first year, I was getting pretty good at reading each slip of paper containing an announcement for a club, sport, or the daily lunch offerings. I could actually be looking at the next announcement and still be reading the last sentence from the previous one. Most of the time I didn't know the content of what I was reading, I was just reading. My secretary always reviewed them prior to giving them to me to make sure they were readable and appropriate.

Two announcements during my time as high school principal got through the screening process and were read as they were written, causing widespread merriment. One I didn't even pick up as being funny, and the other I caught onto only as I was reading it—which was too late. Both were "set-ups" by faculty members.

The first was an announcement following the conference debate tournament the previous weekend. Monday announcements were always lengthy, sometimes containing over twenty different news items on separate slips of paper. On this day there were approximately fifteen slips and the secretary was absent. I grabbed the pile from her desk basket, went into my office and starting reading. About halfway through the announcements, I read the following:

This past Saturday the debate team came in second at the conference debate tournament held at East High School. Individual first place awards were won by Sally Gruning, Beth Channing, and Phillip Cosgrove. This was the first year that our team did not win the Master Debater award.

Of course there was no such award as the Master Debater. I had been had. And when I read this fast, which I always did to get through the pile—well, try it yourself and see why everyone was laughing. I didn't even know it until the next passing period when some students came up to me in the hall and said, "Way to go!" When I questioned them on what I was being congratulated for, they unabashedly told me what I had said.

The other one, which was also on a Monday about a year later, really was innocent and written by the business computer teacher—who was as strait-laced as they come. Some students had been unscrewing the plastic holder on the bottom of the computer mice and taking the rubber balls out, causing them not to work. She always had replacements but was getting tired of having to deal with this, so she wrote the following announcement that I read as written:

Computer students take note: Whoever is taking the mouse balls out of the computer lab can return them to Mrs. Jarvis and there will be no penalty. Replacing mouse balls is time consuming and interrupts the educational process. Thank you.

I couldn't believe I actually read this, but I did. It was the running joke in school for several days. From that time on we really screened the slips and went to student-read announcements, which was actually better for the kids since they paid closer attention to each slip and shared the responsibilities of screening.

☎ Call from a very upset father:

"Okay, I know you are just the secretary, but I have really had it with the hall monitor at your high school. She asks my daughter Julie for passes all the time, and when Julie says the teacher didn't give her one she sends her back to the class or to the office. Obviously the teacher knows she is out of the class since she isn't there. Please have the hall monitor call me to explain why she has to ask her for passes all the time?"

WINDOW ON A SOUL

A message as mysterious and poignant as a note in a bottle.

Over the years I have intercepted many notes written by kids—in study halls, in books, on desks, just about everywhere you can imagine. Kids think that adults in school don't read or care about these notes, but we often do. The notes typically fall into two categories: love notes between a boyfriend and girlfriend or cute notes from girl friend to girl friend. Some talk about how much someone dislikes this person or that teacher. Many are funny, some juvenile. Some very graphically describe a serious boyfriend/girlfriend relationship.

Most of these notes are written on white lined paper torn from a spiral notebook. No matter what the contents of the notes or the type of paper used, most have one thing in common that makes them easy to spot: they are folded over many times!

When I was a high school principal in a suburban school district, there was a twenty-minute locker clean-out exercise at the end of each semester. Students would discard the mounds of paper often to be found at the bottom of their lockers. (One side benefit was the discovery of "stolen" or otherwise vanished library books beneath the mess in the lockers.) At the end of each locker bank was a fifty-gallon garbage container. Since much of the paper never made it into the containers, the halls would be littered with paper until swept.

I enjoyed walking the halls during these frenetic clean-out exercises, visiting with kids, watching them do battle with their lockers, laughing with them, helping them, and just being part of the activity. I also liked helping the custodians clean up after the kids went back to their classes, and they always appreciated the help. Most of my time was spent in the senior hall since I was their advisor as well as their principal.

It was during one of these clean-outs, between first and second semester, that I found what I consider to be one of the warmest and most eloquent notes I have ever read. I do not know who wrote it, nor do I know the recipient, nor do I know if the author was a boy or a girl. There were no clues to any of that anywhere on the note. I have always assumed it was written by a student since it was part of the locker clean-out trash. All I know is that it contains some very sincere and warm feelings from one person to another. The note was on yellow lined paper and it reminded me so much of part of my childhood. Here is the note as I found it in the hallway:

> *This note represents some of my most sincere and deepest thoughts. I never have been able to communicate with anyone my most private thoughts and my most sincere emotions. With you it feels like I have known you since I was that little child you referred to. It seems that you have known me or about me before I even talked to you. Your responses to anything I say are wonderful, honest, helpful, insightful, and warm.*

> *I used to have a blanket and later on a coin that I kept with me every night when I went to bed. It is the only thing I can clearly remember in my childhood. This blanket represented everything in my life that was "safe." I kept it even in pieces and rags until my mom threw it away without telling me when I was in fourth grade. When I held it, I felt safe. When I held it, it soaked up my tears and helped me drift away to sleep. To me the word "safe" is a word that is almost sacred. "Safe" means never having to worry about or fear for a loss of affection, loss of caring, loss of loving, or loss of the feeling of security. I have never used this word or was able to define it until I met you. "Safe" equals you.*

> *In the quiet of my life, my happiness and new look at life through the window you created in my mind centers on the*

"safe" feelings and security that you have brought into my life. "Safe" is wonderful. "Safe" is that little child holding your hand and looking into your beautiful eyes. I have never been as happy and content in my life as I am now. If I could see you every day it would be great, but I must make the best out of what we have, which is wonderful. This is my special message to you.

I miss you so much.

I kept this note tucked away in my 1987 planner and have read it periodically over the years. I found this note to be very deep in thought and emotion and at the same time so simple. I have wondered about the person who wrote it. I, too, had a blanket as a young child and remember how special it was to me. When I hear the word "safe," my mind drifts away to this note.

Being "safe" is essential to our lives and sometimes we take it for granted. This student did a remarkable job of defining "safe" in his or her own world, a sentiment we all might wish for in each of our worlds— and especially wish for each other.

☎ Call from a parent about school being cancelled:

"I heard on TV that there is no school today. Is that true and why?" This call came in to a secretary at 6:05 a.m. The secretary asked the parent if she had looked outside and noticed the whiteout snow storm, to which the parent replied that she was still in bed but could hear the wind!

THE CASE OF THE MISPLACED MUMMY

Maybe this is what happened in Egypt so long ago. . .

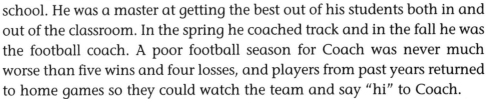

Coach was a middle-aged man whom everyone loved. His laugh was contagious and he had a way of making all his students feel just great about being in school. He was a master at getting the best out of his students both in and out of the classroom. In the spring he coached track and in the fall he was the football coach. A poor football season for Coach was never much worse than five wins and four losses, and players from past years returned to home games so they could watch the team and say "hi" to Coach.

Coach was the taskmaster and made the hard calls with the team. He disciplined players when they needed it, he called the offensive plays, and he's the one who took on disgruntled parents who were unhappy with their sons' lack of playing time. Coach's first assistant coach, Larry, was the person in whom the kids could confide or seek out if things weren't going as expected, especially when they had found themselves on the business end of a few pithy words from Coach and were upset. Larry was that special kind of person who could just listen and understand, and the players would do just about anything for him.

Traditions loomed large in the way Coach approached his work, and the Thursday practice before the last Friday football game of the year was always special indeed. Larry was the central focus of one special "last Thursday" football tradition: the annual first assistant coach ritual mummifying.

So it was on this particular "last Thursday" that the seniors called the team together under the bright lights of the main field in the gathering dusk and, in their last big moment of practice glory as seniors, gave short, rousing talks to fire up the players for the last game and the play-offs. At the end of this hot-headed huddle, the team sent up a huge cheer and started running toward the locker rooms. The seniors, though, as long-standing tradition demanded, lagged behind as everyone else left the field, and lay in wait for Larry to finish briefing the managers and for the managers to leave. The moment they did, as Larry gathered the last bits of equipment and coach stuff, the seniors descended on him like a pack of jackals, picked him up, and carried the struggling—if laughing—Larry to the fifty yard line, dead in the center of the field. The big field lights started shutting off in sequence around the field as unseen hands threw switches somewhere.

As had been the convention for ten long years of this lighthearted nonsense, Larry tried to fight them off and escape but to no avail. The seniors assured him that he was simply the greatest—then used about ten rolls of white athletic tape to bind him up firmly in the spitting image of a mummy.

As this "mummy" sat at midfield in the last of the twilight, his wrapped body shaking with muffled laughter, all the seniors stood around and loudly sang the school song, then ran off to the locker room, leaving poor mummified Larry sitting alone and helpless in the growing darkness of night.

Of course this proud tradition included somebody's coming to rescue the mummy. That task fell to Coach. Every year as everyone left the locker room, Coach would say goodbye to the last player, then head off dutifully down to the field with the tape scissors and cut Larry loose.

However, on this particular Thursday night, as Larry sat waiting patiently on the field to be freed, as everyone left the locker room except the equipment manager, Coach was occupied with a serious equipment problem that simply had to be handled before the next night's big game. He was watching the equipment manager repair the equipment when the phone rang. It was Coach's wife wanting to know where in the world he was, since he was already supposed to be meeting her at a birthday party! He had completely lost track of the time! He hung up and grabbed his coat just as the equipment manager signaled success on the little crisis. The two left the locker room and drove away.

Coach had to turn on his wipers as he drove off quickly toward the birthday party rendezvous with his wife; it had begun to drizzle.

And Larry sat waiting patiently on the pitch-black football field, sealed from head to sole in white tape, wondering when Coach was going to arrive with the tape scissors.

I was just sitting down to eat dinner when Larry's wife called my home at about 7:00 p.m. wondering if I had seen him. I was immediately concerned and perhaps a little alarmed. She, of course, knew what day it was and that practice would run a little late. She even expected Larry to come home laughing about being taped up as usual. But she was beginning to worry since he was later than usual. She had called Coach's house, but no one was home. I told her I would look into it and let her know.

The drizzle had turned to a steady rain and with the temperature hovering around fifty degrees, there was a definite chill in the air. I could see my breath when I stepped outside. I drove to the football field. As I approached, I could see that the field was entirely dark, all the lights out, no signs of anyone anywhere. I parked my car next to the locker room and went inside, but it, too, was dark, and there was no one around.

Something compelled me to go look at the field itself, even though the lights were all off and it was completely silent. As I stepped to a vantage point looking onto the playing field, even in the dark and the rain, I could see what unmistakably was a whitish lump in the center of the field. That's when I heard very muffled hollering for help. I sprinted, splashing, to midfield and assured Larry that he soon would be released. I ran, splashing, back to the locker room, scavenged around and managed to find tape scissors, then dashed back out to the sloppy, wet field.

When I got there, to Larry's credit he was actually laughing, even though the poor man had been sitting in the cold rain for an hour. He was drenched.

Well, sometimes Coach just forgot things. This time, what he forgot was Larry. And this time, Larry said, he was going to return the favor. He told me he was fine to drive home, so we parted with my apologizing to him—on behalf of the whole world, I guess.

About 9:00 p.m. that night, as Larry was finally getting himself dry and warm at home, he had his wife call Coach and ask where Larry was. She agreed to play along, telling Coach that she was terribly worried about Larry, since he hadn't yet come home from practice and hadn't called her, which was very, very unusual for Larry.

The call had all the effect Larry could have hoped for: Coach just about choked on the phone, suddenly realizing full well that he had gone off and left Larry sitting on the field. Stumbling all over himself, though, Coach just told Larry's wife that he would, uh, check on something and call her right back.

Coach lived about 800 yards from the field. He got there in less than two minutes. He found himself staring at a huge dark empty wet field. Larry was nowhere to be seen. Coach ran everywhere, even checking even to see if Larry had rolled under the bleachers for cover from the rain. Larry was not there. Coach dashed to the nearest phone, in near panic now, and frantically called Larry's home trying to figure out what he was going to tell Larry's wife. He had to tell her the truth!

The phone rang twice, before Larry answered. There was a long silence. Coach said, "Larry?" And Larry burst out laughing.

Poor breathless Coach was now also speechless. When he found his tongue again, he kept apologizing over and over to Larry.

Of course the story grew the next day at school and soon, Larry had actually spent the night on the field, and the only wonder is that the gossip factory didn't build a pyramid around him. The players were a little worried that it was true that he spent the night out in the rain. Larry, of course, wanted them to concentrate on the game that night, not the mummy escapade, so by lunchtime, he had explained the truth to everyone.

Whether fortunate or unfortunate, that was the end of the mummy tradition. The superintendent and school board became concerned that someone could actually have been hurt and asked me to tell Coach to end the practice.

Always a man of few words, Coach just said, "Yeah, I guess that about wraps it up."

Jenny's teacher seems to be getting really cranky lately. I know she is eight months pregnant, but Jenny says she is just always upset when Jenny pushes kids at recess who push her first. We let Jenny stay home yesterday so she would understand that you need your rest when you are pregnant.

FULL CIRCLE

A ring and destiny.

In the fall of 1964 I was a member of the high school football team, playing first team defensive end and second team offensive end. One particular Saturday afternoon game was probably the worst weather conditions we had ever experienced. It was cold and raining so heavily that we could barely see the sidelines through the entire game. The puddles on the field were like miniature ponds. The footing was terrible, and the only way our team won that game (by over forty points) was that the other team simply played worse than we did. My girlfriend was in the stands that day, unable to keep from getting drenched, even though she had brought a big umbrella.

When I was in high school, boys often would give their girlfriends their class rings to wear. Typically, the girls had to wrap angora around the back of the ring so it would fit their smaller fingers and stay on securely. Wrapped though it might be, this ring thing was no meaningless ritual to most; it carried a great deal of significance. Then, school rings were 14-carat gold, and the parallels to marriage traditions can hardly go unnoticed: it really represented a bond of hearts, a loyalty to each other, that "practice marriage" state called "going steady." I was proud to have given my girlfriend my ring to wear.

The "mud bowl" I was playing in that day wore on to its final messy conclusion, and we dragged ourselves—even in victory—toward the waiting team bus, soaked, cold, and mainly wretched.

That day, we were to return to school to shower and change. Sitting in a soaked uniform, I remember thinking that the bus ride home on that cold, rainy Saturday seemed to take forever. Even after changing into warm clothes, I couldn't escape the chill that penetrated my bones as I waited for my girlfriend to meet me in the school parking lot, wondering what possibly could be taking her so long.

When she finally arrived she was in tears. Miserable, inconsolable, she explained that she was late because she had lost my class ring while at the game. I was stunned. The angora had gotten wet and the ring must have slipped off without her noticing. She had searched everywhere, soaking wet, sinking deeper and deeper into despair, and finally had to give up and come get me. The next day we went back to the stadium and searched, but we never did find the ring.

It was an awful sense of loss. I did what I could to keep her from feeling guilty about it. It was just one of those really unfortunate things that life seems to dish out.

More than twenty years later, in 1985, I was a high school principal, sitting in my office at my desk doing paperwork when the phone rang. It was a secretary who worked at the high school I had attended. I could not imagine why she was calling me. Then she asked me if I had lost my class ring at a neighboring high school over twenty years ago. It was one of those moments in life where you suddenly are transported in time, where you practically are in that exact past moment, senses alive, experiencing the cold, the rain, the mud, and the despair and loss.

Dazed, I said yes, I had, and heard her explaining that the old stadium where we had played that long-ago day was being renovated, and that a bulldozer operator digging out the footings under the old stadium had happened to see something glitter. He got down from his dozer and found a class ring. Since it had the school's name on it, he mailed it to the office. The secretary had noticed that it belonged to someone in the class of 1965 with the initials of DRJ. She had then looked in the alumni directory and discovered that I was the only person in that class with those initials, and she had tracked me down.

I looked at the phone in disbelief. This was so surreal. I never had dreamed in my wildest flights of imagination that I would ever see the ring again. I thanked her in the most adequate way I could muster, and she seemed very pleased to have found the ring's home.

She mailed the ring to me, and when I opened the envelope, still with a sense of "this just can't be," I found there in it my high school ring from twenty long years before. With the exception of a scratch on the stone, it looked almost brand new.

Perhaps the story should end there. It certainly was a rewarding end to a very strange journey for that ring. But the ring hadn't fulfilled its entire purpose yet, and maybe that's why it was returned to me.

In 1990, I was a superintendent of schools and the time was approaching for my oldest son to purchase his own class ring. He came home one day and told me that the ring company had a special program: if your parents had a class ring that was 14-carat gold, they would weigh the ring and give a credit towards the purchase of a new class ring for the child. I smiled at my son, remembering what my own class ring had meant to me so long ago, and thinking about the strange trip it had taken to come back to me. Though of course there was a sentimental attachment to it, I thought that now I maybe understood why it had found its way home. I went to where it was stored, gave the ring a long look, then handed it over to my beaming son to take in for appraisal. The ring company offered an even trade, and I decided that it simply must have been that ring's destiny.

My son wore his new class ring with great pride. It closed the circle for me to see it on his finger. I don't think, though, that he ever gave it to a girlfriend to wear.

☎ Call from an upset football booster:

"Just because it is 102 degrees doesn't mean that the football team can't practice as hard as any other day. I heard the coach cut practice short due to the heat. When I was a player we just ate salt pills and they wouldn't even let us have any water. We were much tougher then. What is the phone number of the school board president?"

ALIENS IN THE BATHROOM

Boys discover life in their pockets.

Little boys know how to have fun in the bathrooms. They are not at all inhibited and like to play with water, towels, and even deodorizing urinal cakes.

Brian and Charles were typical first grade boys. One morning, as they were in the restroom making noises, laughing, and giggling, a teacher's assistant heard them as she walked by the bathroom entrance, so she opened the door a little and told them to finish using the bathroom and get back to their classroom.

At this point Brian and Charles just giggled more, if not even a little louder. Once again, the assistant told the boys to finish using the bathroom and get to their classroom or she would have to come in and see what they were doing. If teacher's assistants or classroom teachers suspect mischief, they will go into the bathrooms, though simply announcing that they will come in usually stops any monkey business. But not this time. The boys just continued laughing.

The assistant entered the boys' bathroom. All of a sudden the boys became very quiet, each standing in front of separate urinals going to the bathroom. She asked the boys what was so funny and why they didn't listen to her first request for them to finish up and get back to their classroom. Brian was the first to speak and he said, "Charles touched my alien."

Deciding that this situation was one for the principal to deal with, the assistant told the boys to zip up their pants and come with her to the office. First graders get pretty scared when they are in trouble and, in this case, Brian and Charles quit smiling and walked very quietly with the assistant to the office.

Once in Principal Rathburn's office, the assistant had the boys sit in the anteroom and went into the office to relay to Principal Rathburn what she had observed and had been told in the boys' bathroom. Mr. Rathburn thanked the assistant and sent her on to her duties, then went to the outer office where Brian and Charles were seated, looking sheepish and as innocent as possible.

Mr. Rathburn asked Brian to come into the office. He told Charles to wait outside, that he would speak with him later. Brian sat in the chair across from Mr. Rathburn's desk and asked, "Am I in trouble?" Mr. Rathburn closed the door, told Brian to relax and tell him what had happened in the restroom with Charles.

Brian rushed it all out in a blurt. At first they were just having fun playing with water and paper towels and then Charles touched his "alien" and that's when the assistant came into the bathroom and Brian told her what had happened and so—and so—and so she took them to the office.

Mr. Rathburn asked Brian whether he wanted Charles to touch his "alien" and Brian said no. Mr. Rathburn asked Brian to remain in his office so he could go and talk to Charles.

In the outer office Charles was by now very quiet and sort of pale. Mr. Rathburn invited Charles into the small conference room next to his office so they could talk alone. There, Charles gave the same account to Mr. Rathburn as Brian had, but added that Brian also touched his "alien." Mr. Rathburn asked Charles if he had wanted Brian to touch his "alien" and Charles said no.

It wasn't unusual for first grade students to explore their bodies, but it was also a situation that needed to be reported to their parents so that when the boys went home from school there was no question about what had taken place.

Mr. Rathburn took Charles to his office where Brian was anxiously waiting for him to return. Both boys were very quiet as they waited for Mr. Rathburn to say something. Being the veteran principal that he was, he wanted to keep this situation as calm as possible and not upset the boys. So he said to Brian, "Charles said you touched his 'alien' too, Brian. Is that true?" Brian looked down and said yes. Mr. Rathburn then said that he was going to have to call their parents and both boys became teary-eyed.

"Okay boys," he said, "I don't want you to be upset, but do you remember what you have learned about 'good touching' and 'bad touching' this year in class?" Both boys solemnly nodded yes. He then asked, "Do you think touching each other's 'aliens' would be good or bad touching?" With that question, both boys perked up, put their hands in their pockets and pulled out small, green, plastic alien creatures and gave them to a very shocked Mr. Rathburn.

At that point Mr. Rathburn's big challenge was to keep himself from bursting into laughter—which he somehow did quite admirably.

Note from a first grade parent:

We will be gone this Friday to attend an anniversary for our parents. Candy will miss her phonics lesson, and we are wondering if we can take the "g" cut-out letter with us so she can practice in the car. We will practice the "g" sounds a lot. Thank you.

THE PHANTOM

Haunting the not-so-hallowed halls.

Help me, let me out of here!

Holiday seasons are always a very busy time of the year in schools, but high school faculties generally aren't as caught up in the holiday festivities as are elementary faculties. One year, while I was a high school principal, I decided that there simply was no good reason in the world for us to be missing out on the fun. And that is when "The Phantom" first appeared at our high school—not at Halloween, but in the hectic weeks leading up to the big Christmas/New Year holidays. If Scrooge could have Marley's ghost, why couldn't we have a capricious visitation or two?

I decided to establish a tradition, but one that would be a closely guarded secret among the chosen few. I laid out my wickedly mischievous plot for two outstanding teachers with wonderful senses of humor, then swore them solemnly to secrecy.

The first evidence of "The Phantom" soon appeared mysteriously: a simple list of every faculty member—including "The Phantom" co-conspirators—on the refrigerator in the teachers' lounge. The title of the list was "Happy Holidays from The Phantom." The list merely contained the names of the faculty members in alphabetical order with an empty box next to each name. No explanation or other information was included. The list just hung there, stirring faculty curiosity.

The goal of "The Phantom" was equally simple: to play an appropriate and good-natured practical joke on every faculty member in the high school before school let out for the holidays. My two accomplices and I split the faculty into thirds so we could accomplish the task within the school days in December. Every practical joke had to be reviewed and approved by all three of us so nothing would get out of hand. All of our planning took place before or after school. Once a faculty member had fallen victim to "The Phantom," a star was placed in the box next to his or her name on the refrigerator.

In order to complete our joke schedule, we knew we would have to pull off at least two practical jokes each day. Some jokes were the quick-and-easy variety, and some took a few days to fully implement. The faculty members who had fallen prey to "The Phantom" began to notice that there was a star next to their name on the list in the lounge, and the game was afoot! The list became the center of attention each morning and during each lunch period. "Who will be next?" was the topic of conversation as the victims shared what had happened to them. It was amazing to see the effect this basically simple game was having on often serious, sometimes even dour, educators. We all found ourselves laughing and giggling like kids—secret perpetrators and victims alike.

The best joke to my mind was the one we played on Betsy, an English teacher who had first period planning. She taught research and writing classes and her classroom was right next to the media center with a door leading to it. She was an outstanding teacher but very strict on details, and she really made the college-bound kids toe the mark.

Betsy had a predictable daily routine. Arrive at school about 7:30 a.m. Prepare her classroom and check in with the media center director, too. Greet students on arrival and help with homework. Check her mailbox, return to classroom, close her door, and use first period for final planning. It was this routine that led us to the best of all our practical jokes.

On a cassette tape, we recorded a high-pitched voice pleading, "Help me, let me out of here." It was recorded every nine minutes for forty-five minutes. The tape was silent between recordings but continued to play until the next "Help me, let me out of here." After Betsy had left school one day, we placed a battery-operated tape player in the ceiling in her classroom hidden by a tile and the air return. The voice on the tape could easily be heard anywhere in the room.

The next morning when Betsy went to the office to check her mailbox, one of my two cohorts, whose room was right next to Betsy's, went into her classroom, pushed up the tile and started the tape player. Betsy returned to her classroom and closed the door. We waited.

But Betsy reported nothing to the office about any hearing any voices or sounds.

The next day, "The Phantom" followed the exact same pattern.

Again, Betsy did not say a word to anyone.

We were really scratching our heads. So after Betsy left school that afternoon, we let ourselves into her classroom and checked the tape player to make sure it was working properly. It worked perfectly. We went home a little perplexed, but we needn't have been.

The following morning, a Wednesday, when I came to work, I found Betsy in my office. Rather hesitantly, she said, "I have something very unusual happening in my room. Could you come down and listen to it with me?" I screwed my face into a mask of concern and said of course. I asked her to excuse me just a few moments while I took care of some pressing business.

I hastily located a co-Phantom who rushed off to sneak into Betsy's classroom and turn off the tape player.

Returning to gather Betsy, I lollygagged as I walked with her through the halls to her classroom. Once inside, she finally explained to me the problem: no matter what I thought about it, she absolutely knew that she had heard a very faint, high-pitched voice saying, "Help me, let me out of here," frequently during her first period planning for two days in a row. She said that first hour was the only time of the day she heard the voice. I furrowed my brow deeply and told her that I would stay in her room to listen with her.

Of course nothing happened. I walked around the classroom. I asked Betsy where the sound had been coming from, and she said it was very hard for her to tell. I said, "Mmm."

After a while, a little red-faced, she thanked me for coming to her room and said she would let me know if it continued.

The next morning Betsy again came to the office and again asked me if I would please come to her classroom to listen for the voice. So again I went with her to her room, and, of course, there was no voice.

Betsy was getting exasperated. "I'm not making this up and I know you think I am dreaming or something, but seriously, there is a voice saying, 'Help me, let me out of here,' and it happens about every ten minutes." I sat and waited with her for another twelve minutes, but of course nothing happened.

Finally, gently slapping my hands on my knees, I stood, smiled, and I told her that if she heard the voice again on Friday morning, we would ask the media center director to bring in a tape recorder to record the voice. Betsy was sort of chewing on her lower lip, but thanked me very kindly for my help.

We decided it was time for a merciful end. We did not run the same tape on Friday; we made a new recording with the same high-pitched voice saying, "Thank you for letting me out of here—this is 'The Phantom'." A star was posted next to Betsy's name during her planning period.

She came storming down to the teachers' lounge, trying so hard to be angry, but was laughing far too much to pull it off. She regaled every faculty member she could collar with the story, pointing out how her star had mysteriously appeared to prove it. Two of The Phantoms were in the teachers' lounge as Betsy recounted the story to each teacher who entered the room, so we got to enjoy the fruits of our labors first-hand. And, of course, like all good stories, it grew in the telling—although your humble narrator, here, is giving it to you straight.

Betsy claimed that this practical joke was the funniest thing that had ever happened to her. Her husband even wrote a note to "The Phantom" with congratulations on a job well done—which Betsy posted next to the victims' list on the refrigerator.

"The Phantom" continued to haunt our not-so-hallowed halls every December, striking mock-terror into the hearts of all, until I moved to another school district. The faculty began to look forward to the first school day in December, when the list would be posted on the lounge refrigerator. And they never caught the poster posting it. The identity of "The Phantom" was never revealed. Some thought they knew who "The Phantom" was, but no one ever really knew for sure. To this day, two of the Phantoms still remain anonymous. Only I have been reckless enough to give myself away.

☎ Concerned parent call:

"Please tell whoever delayed the start of school today by two hours that this is just crazy. We just plowed out our driveway to the main road and it only took an hour. Why not delay school for just one hour?"

AGELESS COURAGE

The strength and resiliency of the heart can't be measured in years.

Our middle school was a sixth, seventh, and eighth grade structure. Kids go through three pretty trying years in middle school. We used to joke that feet and hormones pretty well described kids at this age. Unlike an elementary principal who has kids in a building for six years, a middle school principal only has them for three years. Having Joey as a student in my building for three years was truly a blessing.

Joey came to sixth grade as a very bright, yet quiet youngster. He lived with his mother and grandfather, his father having died when he was only one year old. Joey had curly blonde hair and glasses and a slight build. Reading was one of his passions, and often we would find him sitting in the library media center lost in a book long after the rest of the kids had cleared the building.

Joey's grandfather often picked him up from school, and the faculty and staff got to know him pretty well, because quite frequently, he would have to enter the school in search of Joey, who would once again be sitting in the library, absorbed in his reading, having lost track of time.

Sometimes his grandpa would come to the office and chat with the school secretary. If I was in my office, I would visit with him for a while and then we would walk to the library together. Grandpa always had a story about growing up in the area and was curious to know if I knew this person or that person.

Upon hearing his grandpa's voice, Joey's face would light up. He would run to greet his grandpa and they would laugh together about Joey once again losing track of time. Then, with his grandpa's arm around his shoulder, Joey would retrieve his things from his locker and they would walk out to the car, chatting and joking and laughing.

Joey's mother was a great mom. She always dropped Joey off at school in the morning on her way to work. She never missed a parent/teacher conference and always spent time helping Joey each evening. On weekends I would frequently see Joey and his mom at the city library. Education was important to her, and it was very evident that she and Joey were a close team.

During the winter of Joey's sixth grade year, his mom came for a private visit to tell me that Grandpa had been diagnosed with cancer. My heart sunk at the news, and I choked back tears to hear that his condition was deteriorating rapidly. Joey had been told and was, she said, pretty scared. Grandpa had done his best to assure Joey that dying was part of life and that Joey and his mom would be fine when he had moved on. She wanted the school counselor to be aware of the situation, and she promised to keep me informed as her father's cancer progressed.

The school counselor soon talked with Joey about his grandpa's cancer. Joey really didn't want to talk to her about it but asked if he could see me. A good counselor realizes that children are sometimes closer to a particular teacher or, in this case, the principal. She and I set up a schedule for Joey and I to talk each week or as often as he needed.

Joey would come to my office and just sit and tell me that he was really going to miss his grandpa when he died and that he was most worried about his mom. I did more listening than talking with Joey. Sometimes there really isn't much to say, but being there for kids, really caring, really listening, helps them talk things out.

March came and Joey's mom called to say that her father was now very ill and that any day could be his last. She was a strong woman and tried to show little emotion. Joey had expressed his desire to her to stay in school and go to the hospital only when things got to the point where his grandpa's time was very short. We decided that his mom would call me when the time came, and I would get Joey out of class and have him ready for her to pick up.

The day Joey's mom called came all too soon. I walked down the hall to Joey's math class, stood quietly at the door, and motioned for him when he saw me. He got right up from his seat and gathered his books, and we walked down the hall together to his locker. While he was not crying out loud, tears were seeping from his eyes and streaming down his cheeks. He looked up at me, thanked me for being there, and assured me that he would be okay. I managed to smile the best I could and we walked to the door to look for his mom. I silently put my arm on his shoulder and he rested his head on my side until his mom arrived. He said goodbye and ran to the car.

I watched them drive off, thinking what a brave twelve-year-old he was. I was thankful that I had been given the opportunity to be there for him. And Joey was there for his grandpa when he died.

Joey returned to school a few days later and finished his sixth grade year with straight "A's." He still lost track of time reading in the library. Seventh grade was not too much different for Joey except his voice dropped and he started to fill out as most kids do at some time in middle school. He still was a straight "A" student and entered many writing and poetry contests. He won many of these, and his name was frequently in the daily announcements for these honors.

It was a few weeks prior to the start of Joey's eighth grade year when his mom came once again to see me privately. She had been diagnosed with cancer and was starting chemotherapy. She had told Joey. He was very worried and didn't even want to start the school year. I asked whether she needed a family counselor to help Joey and she said they were seeing their priest and it was going fine. Her main concern was Joey's reluctance to start school. She asked if I could I help. We made plans for Joey to come to school the week prior to classes so I could visit with him.

I decided to offer Joey a "job" as one of the eighth grade students who read the daily announcements over the intercom and also as the office runner during his third period study hall. I always explained to the student office runners that they could study during this time and only had to do errands when needed. This seemed to help move Joey toward a willingness to attend school; he thought being an office runner would be great as long as he had study time. I also told Joey that his mom had told me about her cancer. Joey had openly talked with me about his grandpa's cancer, but he would not talk about his mother's condition. He thanked me for being concerned and then said he would see me the first day of school.

The school counselor informed Joey's eighth grade teachers about his mom's situation and requested that they report any changes in Joey as the year progressed.

Joey loved doing the daily announcements and was our best office runner. He studied most of this time, but he also used this time, at least occasionally, to talk about his mother and ask me questions about her condition. I called his mother to inquire about her health and let her know that Joey was still doing well in school but had begun to talk about her cancer and ask questions that we really couldn't answer. She explained to me that her cancer had spread and that it was a very dangerous lymphoma type of cancer. She and her brother had started making arrangements for Joey to live with him if anything were to happen to her. An attorney was drawing up the legal papers and setting up a trust fund for Joey. I asked whether Joey was aware of the seriousness of her condition. She explained that at the next session with their priest they were going to talk through the entire situation.

I was just sick in my heart when I hung up the phone. I could hardly move. Losing his grandpa had been difficult for Joey, but losing his mom would be a devastating loss and shock. I forced myself into action. I spoke to the counselor, and we had a team meeting with Joey's teachers to make sure we were all on the same page in trying to help Joey in his time of need.

After the meeting with their priest, Joey's mom called me and said that Joey hadn't said anything at all during the session. When they got home, Joey just sat next to her and cried. Her most recent tests indicated that, at best, she would only have about two months left to live. He would not leave her side and didn't want to go to school. He only wanted to be with her. She was at a loss as to what to do. I asked her if I could talk to Joey about this and, with her permission, set up a different schedule for him. She agreed and brought Joey to school the next day.

Joey was very quiet in our meeting. We agreed that it would be best for Joey to be at school at least three days a week. Monday, Wednesday, and Friday was the plan unless something special was scheduled to take place on the other two days. Joey thought he could keep up with his schoolwork and would give it a try. He really didn't want to come to school at all, but he knew that this was best.

The next month Joey was able to keep up in all of his classes. He told me that his mom was getting a little weaker every day and that his uncle was spending a lot of time at his house helping out as needed. Joey liked his uncle, who had two kids a little younger than Joey.

At the start of the second month, Joey's Mom had to be admitted to the hospital. Joey's uncle came to school and told us that she was slipping fast and could die at any time. He said that he felt it was better for Joey to be in school during the day and that he would take Joey to the hospital every day after school. If anything changed during the day, he would call school and we would get Joey ready to leave at once.

I remember thinking back to Joey's grandfather's situation and hoping things didn't happen again during the school day. Joey and I visited often during the next week. He was very scared, and just talked about anything, just to be talking, especially during his office time.

The next Monday we were talking in the outer office when the call came from Joey's uncle.

I hung up the phone and asked Joey into my office. He knew immediately and just looked at me and started crying—the uncontrollable, sobbing type of crying where you can't catch your breath. I asked the secretary if she would please get Joey's coat from his locker. When she returned, Joey and I went to the door to wait for his uncle.

There was little to say. I had my arm on his shoulder and he was leaning on my side, still crying. At last his uncle arrived. Joey just looked up to me and said, "Thanks for being with me—I love you." Then he gave me a hug and ran to the car.

As I watched him get in the car, I couldn't help crying. I could not even imagine what he was feeling and I thought about what a lot it was for a young boy to go through in his middle school years. But I realized fully then that courage simply cannot be measured in years.

I attended the visitation and funeral. Joey returned to school the next week. He had always been a quiet boy, and perhaps he was a little quieter the rest of the year. But he still loved doing the daily announcements and working third period as our office runner. Academically, Joey kept his "A" average, and in spite of all he had been through, all he had lost, he ultimately graduated from high school as the valedictorian.

Joey never let these tragic events stop him from succeeding in life: he is currently a successful lawyer in Chicago.

I hear he still loses track of time in libraries.

Note from a middle school parent:

Our daughter Judy was absent yesterday because it was that time of the month and she had gym class and we don't think she should have to dress for gym during this time. The gym teacher doesn't agree. Please not only excuse Judy from school yesterday, but from gym class for the rest of the year as well. If you won't do this, we will get the doctor to write a note for the rest of the year.

CONFETTI
CANNON

Frivolity is the mother of detention.

Our state frequently sold as surplus used and overstock items from one public agency or department to another. As a poorer school district, we made good use of this opportunity all the time for office furniture, file cabinets, and generally anything we couldn't afford to purchase brand new or at a higher price. There were always some great deals. After one particular visit to the surplus center, the assistant superintendent returned with what he considered a true find.

The state had ordered economical electric hand dryers to replace paper and cloth towels for all of the highway rest stops. But there was a problem: the dryers the state received were white instead of an off-white, cream color that they swore they had ordered. The off-white dryers were ordered anew, the white ones were taken to surplus for sale to state-funded agencies. That's how the assistant superintendent had found his bargain.

The hand dryers were installed in all of our schools the next summer, and the towel dispensers were removed. When the kids came back to middle school, they really didn't like them—but, hey, they had been a bargain.

Despite some general grousing, the dryers did have some benefits—so to speak. The fact that they rotated 360 degrees was great for kids who had showered in gym class. By pointing the rotating chrome nozzle upwards, students could dry their hair, and this proved to be a pretty popular usage. The nozzles would often be left pointing in the upward position, and few people bothered to rotate them when drying their hands.

Then somebody got hit with the confetti cannon.

Some enterprising and innovative student had discovered that loading punch-outs from computer punch cards (which were prevalent at the time) into an up-turned dryer nozzle, then pushing the "on" button would shoot this manila confetti all over the hapless button-pusher's hair and clothing and all over the bathroom as well.

Most people wouldn't look at the nozzle before hitting the "on" button, and this "confetti" would be far enough down the nozzle not to be noticed by most, even if they did.

The prankster was having quite a time with this little joke in the boys' bathrooms, and I began getting complaints not only from the confetti cannon victims but from the custodian who had to clean up the messes. We had to stop the pranksters and do something about the blowers in the restrooms to stop this frivolity.

The mysterious cannoneer became quite good at playing this prank. He didn't load a dryer every day. He even snuck into the girls' restroom and loaded one in there, no doubt trying to throw off the hunt. Then he didn't load one for three days. Then he loaded four in one day in three different restrooms. We checked with the faculty that day to see who was issued passes, but there was no clear pattern or a time that would coincide with the times of the blasts in the bathrooms.

On Friday that week, the Fire Marshall stopped by for an annual surprise inspection of the building. As principal, it was my job to take him through the building. About halfway through his visit, we stopped in the restroom to use the facility. A student named Brad was present and I said hello. He was washing his hands and went over to one of the two dyers and to dry his hands. I sort of squinted, hoping he and the Fire Marshall and I wouldn't be subjected to a confetti blast. I was relieved when it was just hot air.

The Fire Marshall finished using the urinal, went over and washed his hands, and before I could even think, he stepped in front of the hand dryer next to Brad and hit the button. The enormous blast of confetti caused him to actually yell out loud and jump back. Brad and I both flinched at the yell.

Then I just put my head in my hand.

Brad said immediately, "I didn't do it!" and I looked up suddenly. I knew at once that, at the very least, he knew *something*. I asked Brad to go to the office, then started trying to explain what had been going on with the dryers to the confetti-covered Fire Marshall, while also trying to help brush him off. To my endless gratitude and relief, he actually laughed about the prank and suggested that we spot weld the nozzles so they could only rotate 180 degrees. That would prevent anyone from loading them.

As I walked him to his car and thanked him for the visit, he was still laughing about the incident. I went directly back to my office, where I discovered that Brad had convinced the secretary that another boy, whom he didn't even know, had entered the restroom while he was in the toilet, and he thought he had heard the person play with the dryer nozzle.

I wasn't nearly as impressed as the secretary. I asked Brad if we could look in his locker. A little color drained out of his face. We marched to the locker and Brad opened it, revealing a brown paper garbage sack half full of the confetti. I gave him a proper principal look with a highly arched eyebrow.

We marched back to the office and called Brad's father at work to tell him about the incident. Brad had explained on the way that his dad worked for an insurance company and that they used these computer cards all the time. His dad brought home the confetti for the kids to use. Brad's dad said that he would not bring any more confetti home and would have a serious talk with his son. After the conversation, I told Brad that he would have detention for a while and that it would be nice if he helped the custodian clean during his detention, as the custodian had been very busy cleaning up after Brad. He sheepishly agreed.

We spot-welded all of those dryers except the ones in the locker rooms where kids really liked to dry their hair. There were no more confetti cannon incidents.

But I can't think of the Fire Marshall's backward leap without a private chuckle.

✏ Note from a parent upset with bus drivers:

"Tell the bus drivers that they are a bunch of chickens. I heard that they are the ones responsible for canceling school today because they thought it was too icy. Just because everyone else called off school doesn't mean we should."

MARCHING TO VICTORY

Beating the drum for a better band image.

In the first month of my first year as a high school principal, one key concern was brought to my attention by the music boosters. The Booster Club had worked closely with the school district and had helped hire one of the best instrumental music instructors in the state to teach at the high school with hopes of turning around the struggling band program. The band was short on players and it seemed as though it didn't receive as much attention as sports, especially football. Members of the Booster Club felt that the central office gave lip service to wanting the music program to be successful, while real support favored the sports programs.

Just like the football team, the band worked hard at putting together a team that was more than the sum of its parts. It required long, hard hours of practice and rehearsal that began three weeks prior to the start of the school year. The band director and I—both new to our jobs there—were keenly aware that in order for the band program to build respect in the school and in the community, it not only had to excel technically, but it needed to gain the support of the athletes and the coaches, since the band and athletic departments were so closely associated in the presentation of sports events. We would have to do some things that were out of the ordinary, so he and I hatched a plan that was carried out in several phases.

Some days later, following a morning practice, the football players came off the field exhausted and hot to find a table set up outside the locker room with a sign that read, "We are proud of you guys. Have some cold juice on the marching band."

It wasn't long before the football coach dropped by my office to tell me the "news" about the band's thoughtfulness toward the team. "In my twenty years as the head football coach, nothing like this has ever happened," he said. He had already told the band director how much he and the team appreciated it. I thanked him for letting me know and allowed myself a private smile as he left my office.

The next week as the marching band came off their practice field, they found a lemonade stand set up in the band room run by three of the football managers with a sign that read, "We'll take care of the first and second half—you guys take care of pre-game and half time. Together we will be the best in the conference." The band students were overwhelmed.

Not only were the two groups building their own teams, they were learning to be a larger team, a team of teams.

The local newspaper was contacted and came to school to take a picture of a few of the football players in their practice uniforms with some of the band students holding their instruments. The article that accompanied the photo talked about this new "team" being forged at the school and explained the new bond that was developing.

This was a good start, major progress in fact. But in the eyes of the student body, it still was not considered "cool" to be in band. Changing this long-standing image would take more than fruit juice and lemonade, and homecoming week seemed to provide an opportunity to break through another "band barrier."

By the time homecoming arrived, the football team had won every game and was rated first in the state. Homecoming week would culminate in a large student and community pep assembly in the gym on Friday afternoon, and, while the focus was football, we wanted to channel some of that enthusiasm into a new and greater appreciation of the talent and skills of our band.

For months, in addition to the normal rehearsals and endless practice that goes with the territory, the band director had been working quietly and separately to build yet another team within the team—a cracker-jack drum line with precision close order drill, thunderous rhythmic cadences, split-second statement-and-answer dialogs between toms and snares, pounding bass drum syncopations, and heart-racing tattoos pounded out in unison and in counterpoint, with wild flourishes of sticks and cymbals and steps. Although some of their repertoire had been seen at a distance during half-time shows, it had only been integrated into the larger band formations. Nobody had seen what they could really do, certainly not up close—not until homecoming, that is.

The student council planning committee had been reluctant to give up ten minutes out of their planned homecoming assembly for a band presentation when the band director and I asked. One went so far as to say, "But they aren't that good and it will detract from the other things we have planned." This earned one of my best silent looks. The band got their ten minutes.

The assembly started as planned. There were rousing speeches and loud stomping and cheers, lots of "pump-up" for the big game, followed by award after award for homecoming events. Then the time came; the cheerleaders announced that there would be a special performance by the band.

There was some cheering, but not much. The band was sitting in its usual section and everyone looked in that direction waiting to hear what they were going to play—but nothing happened. It was quiet.

Then the far doors of the gym opened and the drum line entered in single file, lock step, eyes forward, a single chilling, reverberating, repetitive tap on the side of one drum clicking out the cadence of their otherwise silent precision march to the center of the floor in front of a riveted and hushed crowd. Every person in the drum line was wearing dark sunglasses and backward band caps. They came to a sudden halt in front of the huge crowd of about 1,800 and snapped to face them.

There was a beat of silence. Then all hell broke loose.

No words can capture the experience of a practiced drum corps—the nearly primal thrill of concussive rhythms, the staggering sense of impact and force as a score or more of hands move as one, the flash of twirling sticks and shimmering cymbals and bells, the crash, the thump, the rifle-like report of rim-shot snares. It just raises gooseflesh.

The students leapt to their feet with wild cheers and whistles, dancing, clapping, pounding the benches in time as the drum line stepped and gyrated and beat out rhythms and riffs that echoed almost deafeningly in that big open gym, rhythms that may be as old as mankind, but that certainly reached something in the soul of every person there!

By the time they finished their performance, the entire assembly was screaming, clapping, dancing in the stands, and wanting more—so they did it all again and got the same response.

There was no further "image" problem with the band. That drum line became one of the most requested groups at all assemblies and to this day is still one of the best in the state. The following year the band boosters sold t-shirts with the saying on the front, "The football team will play before and after the MARCHING BAND'S half-time performance." A lot of money was made from the sale of these t-shirts. Even football players bought them!

It's also my understanding that the juice tables are still set up in August.

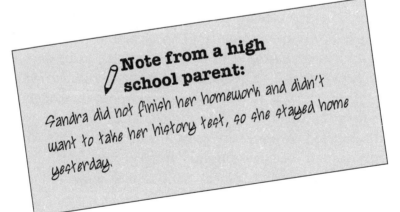

Note from a high school parent:

Sandra did not finish her homework and didn't want to take her history test, so she stayed home yesterday.

SHOWDOWN

There are no teams of prima donnas.

Later in same year that the band got an image face-lift—my first year as a new high school principal—I found myself confronted with another situation related to the band, but this time it was the ugly specter of double standards that extended beyond the walls of the building, beyond the opening and closing bells, out into the community of people whose children we taught, whose support we counted on, and who expected us to instill values in these young people along with academics.

Marching band season culminated with various important contests for bands. The state association sponsored one; the others were run by school districts using the same state format. The district competitions served as a preparation for the state contest and, of course, as a fundraiser for the local school.

At the end of the previous school year, the new band director had held tryouts for the marching band's flag corps, an important part of the competitions. He felt very confident that the fifteen girls finally selected were right for the program and were committed to making it a success. They all had thoroughly understood the participation rules for the performance and practice schedule planned for the year.

One of the important district band competitions was coming up on a Saturday evening. During the intense preparations in the week leading up to it, three of the flag corps girls informed the band director, Mr. Williams, that they wouldn't participate in the Saturday evening contest because they had been invited to another school's homecoming dance and had decided to go.

Mr. Williams reminded the girls that unless they were ill, this was one of the dates that was a requirement of the program. They had signed an agreement indicating that they would be present for the contests or they would be dropped from the corps. They told him that they had talked with their parents and that they were going to go to the dance and didn't think it was fair to be dropped from the flag corps. They didn't consider the district competition important enough to miss out on the homecoming dance where they had friends. Mr. Williams could hardly believe what he was hearing. He pointed out to them that their absence would cause the formations to be off and that the voids would be noticeable. It would affect the scoring at the contest, which wasn't fair to the rest of the band members, all of whom had worked hard to perform well. The girls were not persuaded at all.

Mr. Williams came to me with his dilemma. He knew he had to drop the girls from the corps if they didn't attend the contest, or he would lose all the ground he had gained with his students regarding commitment and responsibility to the program and to their fellow band members. With great effort, a plan was worked out that would allow the girls to perform at 6:30 p.m. at the contest and then go to the other school's dance—albeit late. Mr. Williams presented the idea to them. The girls rejected the proposal.

He was left with no choice: he told all three that they were dropped from the flag corps.

Late that same afternoon, at 5:15 p.m., I was at home getting ready for supper when there was a knock on my door. Imagine my surprise at finding that the superintendent of schools had come to see me.

Perplexed, I invited him in to learn what possibly could occasion such a visit. He told me that parents of the dismissed flag corps girls had contacted him and several school board members, complaining that it was unfair that their daughters were dropped from the program after all the time and effort they had invested in it.

I didn't quite know what to say. Here I was, a first year principal, confronting the superintendent over a question of ethics on which we obviously occupied different sides of the fence.

I took a deep breath, and explained to him the best I could that it was crucial for the school to support the band director the same way we would support any educator—like, for example, a football coach.

I don't think the subtle significance of my carefully chosen example quite hit home, because the superintendent next said that these parents were very influential in the community and could really cause the band program some damage if the action wasn't reconsidered.

I thought about it a minute and decided to make my example not so subtle: I said I would tell Mr. Williams to reconsider under one condition, and the condition was this: if the quarterback on the football team told the coach that he was going to miss the next game so he could go to a homecoming dance at another school, and the coach said the quarterback could go to the dance and yet stay on the team, I personally would reinstate the girls, even over Mr. Williams's protestations.

The superintendent just looked at me for a minute, then said it wasn't a fair comparison.

I smiled politely and asked why.

When he didn't seem to have a ready answer, I'm afraid I seized the opportunity to get on my soapbox. I said that the only thing that wasn't fair was the double standard arising out of favoritism toward sports over the arts, including music and the band. As a new high school principal in only my fourth month in a new district with no real establishment yet in the community, I knew this was a hard position to be taking with the superintendent, and I realized it could have repercussions, but I also knew it was the right position.

The superintendent just looked at me thoughtfully. I gathered courage in that and pressed on. I told him that the band director should never know of this visit, and that he, the superintendent, simply had to tell the board members and parents that the decision was not going to be reconsidered.

We talked a few more minutes and he left. He called the board members and explained that he wasn't going to request reconsideration for the girls. He also called the girls' parents and told them the same thing. Of course, they were furious, but he had already worked out for himself how to deal with that: he suggested the parents attend the next band boosters meeting to explain their frustrations and ask for the rules to be changed.

No parents showed up at a meeting of the band boosters to say they felt that a dance was more important than the band program. That was the end of that.

Although he never knew the full reason why, Mr. Williams was very appreciative of the support from the central office and the board of education. And the band received a Division I ranking at the state contest.

Note from a family going on vacation:

Next week we will be going on our annual vacation. This will involve our fifth grade student Sandy, our ninth grade student Justin, and our senior Brenda. Since we are in the construction business, our winters are the only time we can vacation as a family. We know the ten days that the kids will miss could cause them some academic problems. We would appreciate it if all the teachers would give the kids their assignments ahead of time and they will do what they can before we leave and turn the rest in when we return. You may think that vacations are not educational, but we disagree. We will be in Florida where there are many historic places to visit. If there are any academic penalties for their absences, we will be forced to ask the school board to review these penalties. We wish to avoid any conflicts, as I'm sure you do as well.

THE EGG TIMER

Spontaneous deconstruction? I don't think so.

Most special education teachers have patience beyond belief. One freshman special needs student, Jamie, had proven to be possessed of a downright uncanny ability to pretty much "get to" just about all of his teachers. When it fell to Mr. Benning, one of our best special needs instructors, to take on the precocious Jamie, Mr. Benning vowed not to let the boy "get to him" and was determined to make sure that Jamie was successful in high school.

At the start of the year, Mr. Benning had called Jamie's mother to review his individual education plan and previous problem issues. Most were minor mischief problems that ended up interfering with Jamie's ability to stay in regular classes. Jamie's most serious problem was an almost preternatural inability to tell the truth in situations where he had caused disruptions. Twenty people could have witnessed Jamie do something inappropriate and he would swear unflappably that they were all making it up and that he had done nothing whatsoever.

This could drive any educator almost to paroxysms.

Mr. Benning and Jamie's mother knew that his academic issues were secondary to his casual acquaintance with truthfulness and that if Jamie was going to succeed in high school as well as in society, he had to accept responsibility for his actions. Jamie was included in finalizing a plan with his mom and Mr. Benning that was designed to provide penalties for patent misbehavior and dishonesty. He signed the plan and promised to work harder on those issues.

The first two months of the school year really went well for Jamie. He had only been referred to the office once for talking three times without permission in his English class and since then had been doing his work and staying out of trouble. At his October conference with his mother and Mr. Benning, Jamie reported that he was really feeling great about school and that high school seemed to be a more mature setting, and he wanted everyone to see him as mature.

As the holiday season started to approach, though, Jamie had more difficulty staying focused in class. After Thanksgiving vacation, he was starting to revert back to his old habits and had been referred to the office almost daily. The plan he had signed was implemented as outlined and Jamie didn't like losing privileges both at school and at home as consequences for his actions.

In an effort to get Jamie on a more profitable course, Mr. Benning had come up with a series of special assessment tests that he thought might help Jamie start to focus on potential career interests. The assessment was a battery of academic skills tests matched to career interests. A profile was then generated from the results, comparing the student's interests to his abilities.

Jamie agreed to take the assessment and promised to "really try hard."

The day for the assessment tests came. Mr. Benning explained the assessment to Jamie and explained that each section was timed. He agreed to sit with Jamie and set the kitchen-type egg timer Mr. Benning had brought. Jamie understood that when the timer dinged, he had to put down his pencil. The assessment would take two hours and they decided to start it at 9:00 a.m. since Jamie was always more alert and calm in the morning than the afternoon.

And away they went. I was hoping to hear good news from the assessment.

I was soon surprised to see Mr. Benning arrive at my office with Jamie in tow. Mr. Benning was carrying a test booklet and an envelope that rattled. They both sat down. Mr. Benning explained patiently that as Jamie was taking a timed interest inventory assessment, another teacher stopped by the classroom with a question. Mr. Benning had excused himself, telling Jamie that he was stepping out into the hallway for about five minutes and urged him to continue working, as there were fifteen minutes remaining on the timer for that section.

Mr. Benning stepped out. When Mr. Benning stepped back in, the timer was where he had left it on his desk but not as he had left it on the desk. At this juncture in his narrative, Mr. Benning opened the rattling envelope and emptied its contents onto my desk. The egg timer had been completely disassembled, and all the pieces were lying there: springs, dials, bell, case, and all the little screws.

I stared in amazement and looked to Jamie. When I asked him what happened, he said with great aplomb, "I was taking this test and all of a sudden the timer made a funny sound and shook a little on Mr. Benning's desk and all the parts just started to come off of it. I just kept taking the test until Mr. Benning came back in and then he asked me what happened and I told him the same thing I just told you. Then he said we were going to the office and here we are."

I just kept looking at Jamie and nodding, saying, "Uh-huh, uh-huh." I knew I could not look at Mr. Benning, who was having trouble keeping a straight face.

In a moment of divine inspiration, I asked Jamie if he would empty his pockets for me and he said sure. He put his wallet, some change, and his house keys on the desk. On his key ring was a small screwdriver of the type used to tighten screws on eyeglasses.

I picked it up and studied it, and asked Jamie if there were any possibility—however remote—that instead of a spontaneous deconstruction having miraculously occurred on the desk, he had instead taken the timer apart, screw by screw, with his handy little screwdriver. Jamie tilted his head and he looked at me with an expression on his face that plainly said, "Why would you even ask me a question like that?"

"No," he said emphatically, "it just came apart, just like I said."

Now Jamie was starting to "get to" *me*.

After about another half hour of essentially the same thing, he was *definitely* getting to me! I asked Jamie to stay in my office while Mr. Benning and I stepped outside for a few minutes.

Mr. Benning was having a hard time not laughing out loud as we huddled in the outer office. Despite the frustration, we both had to admire the boy's resourcefulness at finding a way to "get to" almost anyone when that was his aim. We finally hit on a plan of action by which two adult and educated educators might be able to break even with a high school freshman special needs student. Resolved, we marched back into the office in formation.

"Jamie," I announced, "we believe you." Jamie looked at me sideways. "Yes," I went on, "and because we do, we are going to have to send that timer back to the factory for examination and a final ruling on it. Of course, although we believe you, we will have to wait for a report from the factory for a final determination, based on their expert analysis, as to whether you've been telling the truth or not."

Jamie looked puzzled. He asked how long this might take since the holiday vacation was coming up and he didn't want to get into any trouble that would cause him to lose any privileges over vacation. We said that we didn't know since we had never sent in an egg timer to a factory before to find out how it had come apart.

Our answer was allowed to hang in the air for a minute.

Finally Jamie asked, "What happens if I tell you what happened?" Mr. Benning said that the truth was really the most important thing now, and that if Jamie told the truth, Mr. Benning would impose some penalties at school but would not tell Jamie's mother. There would be no home-based privileges lost.

Jamie then confessed that he had been taking the test, when all of a sudden the timer shook and started to clunk and fell over. So he grabbed the timer to stop it from making the noise and then decided that he could fix it by loosening a few screws. When that didn't work, he decided to take it all apart so he would not be distracted. Then when Mr. Benning came back into the room, he decided not to explain the situation and instead told the story he did.

While clearly neither of us thought the timer made any of the noises or fell over as Jamie described, at least Jamie had taken some responsibility for his actions. Mr. Benning was satisfied and they returned to the room to finish the assessment. Mr. Benning afforded me a quick surreptitious wink as he went out the door.

The faculty gave Mr. Benning a gold egg timer that year for Christmas with Jamie's name painted on the side and the year. Jamie is currently a very successful owner of a transportation business in a major city.

Call from a parent upset about school cancellation due to the temperature:

"I can't believe it! There is no snow on the ground, there is no ice, and we just cancelled school because the wind chill index is 50 degrees below zero. I want the superintendent's home phone number, the school board president's home phone number, and the newspaper's complaint line number. This is just too much. Kids can deal with this even if the adults can't."

TEACHERS' HAPPY HOUR

Does the principal have principles?

In 1975 I was twenty-eight years old and was considered young to be a school principal. But somehow I had made it through two years as a middle school principal, and I even began to allow myself to feel that maybe I was getting a handle on things. Fewer of the small things that happened at school were as bothersome to me as they had been in the beginning. I was actually starting to feel some of the cool confidence that I had been walking around attempting to display. The faculty and I had established a very positive working relationship, with even the veteran teachers warming up to this "young guy" as their principal.

I had established Fridays after school as an informal get-together period for the faculty. It was a time when we could congregate in the teachers' lounge to review the past week, share some interesting events and anecdotes, and talk about our weekend plans.

There were usually about fifteen faculty members who stopped in on Fridays. The groups changed from week to week and it was an enjoyable time.

Richard Harding, who was about eight years older than I, was one of our best social studies teachers and was very well-respected by the faculty. Richard never missed a Friday, and he and a few of his friends had the best stories and usually the most fun and interesting plans for the upcoming weekend. He was also a pretty good beer-drinker and made no excuses about how much he really liked beer.

In the lounge, there was an old pop machine. It was the kind you don't see much any more: after you deposited your money, you had to open a long, skinny glass door, grab a metal handle and pull it to the left to release the can.

One Friday afternoon in late fall, I arrived at the school lounge a little later than normal. As I sat down to listen to the conversations that were well underway, Richard announced that he had borrowed the pop machine key from the secretary and, in honor of his recent high bowling score from Tuesday night, had stocked one row of the machine with beer for us to drink. Certain he was kidding, I said, "Very funny, Richard. You know very well that you can't have beer on school property." Laughing, he said, "Sometimes you just have to stretch the rules." He then got up, went to the machine, put his money in, and asked if I wanted to pull the lever.

Still certain that he had to be kidding, I laughed and waved him off. So he opened the skinny glass door, pulled back the handle, and I watched in amazement as a Schlitz beer can came out. I still couldn't come to grips with the fact that Richard was standing in front of me, in the teachers' lounge, in front of other faculty members, holding up a can of beer. He popped the tab and asked me if I wanted a drink.

All I could see were screaming, giant headlines in the local newspaper, "Middle School Faculty Has Beer in Lounge Pop Machine!" I stood up quickly, went over to Richard, and grabbed hold of the can in his hand. He resisted slightly—and the aluminum can collapsed in our grip—just folded in. Everyone in the lounge broke out in laughter.

I knew then that I'd been had.

Once he stopped laughing, Richard confessed that in a Schlitz six-pack he had purchased a few days earlier he had found two cans that obviously were pressurized, but were empty of beer. The machine at the brewery must have gone awry and two cans got through the line without being filled. Richard had cooked up his idea for a practical joke and had gone to my secretary and told her his plan. She agreed to give him the key. My own secretary had helped set me up!

The faculty in the lounge that day had been told of the practical joke before I arrived. Later some told me that they wished they'd had a camera to capture the look on my face when the beer can came out of the machine!

The next Monday, at the end of my weekly meeting with the superintendent, I was getting up to leave when he said, "Say, I understand you had an incident Friday after school that you haven't shared with me yet." Before I became too embarrassed, he started laughing. He, too, had known about it. Richard had called him on the previous Thursday to tell him what he was planning to do, as he didn't want to cause any trouble for me.

I might have still been a little embarrassed as I left, but I also had to smile. I felt I'd been officially initiated all around.

Note from a middle school parent:

Patrick's shop project was not completed, so he and his dad worked on it yesterday since it was due today. Please excuse Patrick and his dad—they were working all day.

THE CALCULATOR

Lessons are learned where they find you—sometimes the hard way.

Teachers are human beings, which is the single most difficult concept for some students and parents to grasp. Many never do. The "teacher mystique" is a potent force that somehow attempts to transform mere mortals into walking, talking paragons of virtue and perfection. It doesn't work, though. We all still have our human frailties, our personal opinions and preferences, sometimes even suppressed prejudices that we don't want to admit even to ourselves and that we make a genuine good-faith effort to leave on the doorstep when the school bell rings.

One such human being was Mr. Franks. In addition to being human, he was a teacher, a good one, who taught physical education. Mr. Franks was saddled with an ambivalence concerning "special needs" or "special education" kids being in his classes at a time when their school day was split between specially trained educators for some subjects and the regular classes for other things—like PE. He disagreed, sometimes vocally, with the concept of the special needs students being mixed into the regular classes and felt that it didn't serve them or anyone well. Mr. Franks kept to himself much of the time, but he was liked all right by most of the staff who could get to know him.

In contrast to Mr. Franks was Mr. Ordant, a very outgoing special needs teacher whose special kids were sent each day to Mr. Franks for their PE classes. Everyone loved him; his special needs kids just adored him. His class comprised the lower functioning group of children in the middle school who had IQs in the mid 80s and who spent most of their time with him in a self-contained classroom. They attended lunch, art, shop, music, and, of course, PE on their own, but all other subject matter was the responsibility of Mr. Ordant.

On more than one occasion, Mr. Franks and Mr. Ordant argued over Mr. Ordant's right, by federal law, to assign "these kids" to PE with the other students. Mr. Franks complied, but it was a struggle. As the middle school principal, there were times I actually had to intervene and set Mr. Franks on the right course to keep everything running smoothly. Sometimes it almost seemed that he would go out of his way to stir up a new argument with Mr. Ordant and me about, as he called it, "this whole mess."

Mr. Ordant did all he could to ease the tension, attending many PE classes and helping Mr. Franks out. He also made sure Mr. Franks knew how much these special needs kids liked him as a teacher and how much he was helping them feel good about themselves.

Despite Mr. Franks's grousing, another side of his nature, a surprising compassion, couldn't help but show through at times. For instance, one of the special needs boys, Blane, came from a home that still had a dirt floor. I learned that Mr. Franks had begun quietly helping Blane by having another set of clothes at the school for him, and that Mr. Franks would do Blane's laundry in the towel room three days a week. Mr. Ordant was very moved at this unexpected gesture of kindness and caring from Mr. Franks.

It might have been this "big brother" attitude toward Blane that caused Mr. Franks to let his usual close guard down one day.

Blane had been working for weeks on a project in shop class, under Mr. Ordant's close supervision. It was a pretty advanced electronics project for someone of Blane's special needs: a switchable converter with a variety of types of plugs that would transform household electrical current to six-volt, nine-volt, or twelve-volt direct current (DC), suitable for powering small electronic things like calculators.

One day in PE Blane told Mr. Franks all about the project, saying that he was almost finished with it, and asked if he could he bring his converter to PE to show Mr. Franks. Mr. Franks of course said yes.

On the day that Blane proudly brought his finished converter to PE class to show Mr. Franks, he happened to be at his desk, figuring his grades on a very expensive calculator. Mr. Ordant was with Blane, whose eyes simply lit up at the magnificent calculator Mr. Franks was using. Blane enthusiastically explained all the details of the converter to Mr.

Franks, taking off the converter's cover for him to see all the soldering Blane had done. But Blane's eyes kept flicking to the calculator sitting on Mr. Franks's desk. Finally, he timidly asked Mr. Franks what voltage his calculator was. They looked on the back. It said "9 volts." Blane's eyes widened, and he hesitated. Then he blurted out excitedly that he wondered if Mr. Franks would plug in his calculator to the converter! Mr. Franks opened and closed his mouth a time or two, then cast a wary eye up at Mr. Ordant.

"Have you tested this thing?"

"Mmmm, no," said Mr. Ordant, but he went on to say that he had supervised the entire process while Blane was building it, and that all the other kids' converters had worked just fine.

Mr. Franks looked again at Blane's beaming, hopeful face. "Fine," he said—though not necessarily with conviction. To Blane's uncontainable delight, Mr. Franks unplugged the calculator's own cord and plugged the converter into the wall. He had Blane set the voltage dial to nine volts and select the correct plug. He tilted the calculator's face a little to make it easier for Blane to see the numbers.

With all systems "go," Mr. Franks finally took the converter plug and slid it into the opening in the back of the calculator.

The red LED numbers lit right up just as brightly as ever!

Then the smoke appeared.

Then the plastic face of the calculator started to melt.

Mr. Franks jerked the converter plug from the wall, and stared in stunned disbelief at his expensive calculator, in mere seconds "transformed" into a smoking, half-melted ruin. He lifted baleful eyes toward Mr. Ordant. Blane just smiled and in the inimitable understatement of innocence said, "Something's not right!"

That broke the tension.

It wasn't long, though, before Mr. Franks appeared in my office and put the carcass of the calculator on my desk, like some relic from a Salvador Dali painting, and asked if the district could buy him a new one. When I got the whole story I had to laugh. He didn't quite share my mirth. Mr. Ordant brought Blane with him and came to the office. He was apologetic, but I told him not to worry about it at all; it was just an honest mistake.

Mr. Ordant told Mr. Franks that the class would replace his calculator, and we all parted friends. And Mr. Franks still did Blane's laundry every week.

He told this story at his retirement party some years later and made it so funny that everyone was in tears! I think Blane taught him some pretty important lessons—not that he ever would admit it in public.

Note from a high school student who had skipped school and wrote his own note:

Yesterday Tom had a stomach ache and stayed home from school. He had to take a lot of Pepto Bismol, which made him sicker. He felt better by the evening and was seen at the shopping mall by his French teacher, but that shouldn't count since school was already out.

CONSCIENCE CRISES

If a small lie extracts a greater truth,
has it been justified?

Chuck was a seventh grade student who came from a low-income family. He was a bright and basically decent kid, but he often had a chip on his shoulder because of his lack of nice clothes, school supplies, and things like that.

In the fall of the school year, a student and his mother came to my office very upset about a brand new Kansas City Chiefs football jacket that had been stolen at school. I asked if the boy's name had been put anywhere in the jacket and was told no. I told the mom that I would watch closely to see if I noticed anyone wearing the coat to school and, if so, I would call her. I then told her son that if he noticed someone wearing his jacket, he should come to me without saying anything to the person.

Usually if kids steal something that is very recognizable, such as a bright red football coat, they won't wear it to school for a while. They will wait until some time passes, hoping that the incident will be forgotten.

Unfortunately, weeks and weeks went by and no coat turned up.

Then one day in the spring of the same school year, the boy who had lost his coat came to my office, stating that he had seen Chuck wearing a red KC jacket to school that morning that looked exactly like the one that had been stolen. I told the boy I'd get back with him, then, not looking forward to the task, I sent for Chuck to come to my office.

Since there was no name in the jacket, I knew it would be hard to get Chuck to admit it if he had, indeed, taken the jacket. When Chuck came to my office I asked him if we could go to his locker to see his KC jacket. He asked why and I told him that one like it was reported stolen in the fall so we needed to clear his name from any suspicion.

We went to his locker and brought the coat back to my office. I looked it over and found that Chuck's name was written on the label in the collar. The jacket was well made. I noticed that it had an inside pocket, and a germ of an idea began to form about how I might get to the bottom of this if I had to, although it presented me with an ethical quandary of my own. Chuck said his mom had purchased it for Christmas and that this was the first day that the weather was nice enough for him to wear it—which I sure had a little trouble trying to add up. He went on to say that plenty of kids owned these kinds of coats and that it wasn't fair for someone to accuse him of stealing it. He suggested that I call his mom to verify that she bought it for him for Christmas.

My hunch was that Chuck wasn't telling the truth. I told Chuck that I didn't need to call his mother if he was being honest, but the truth was that past experience had shown me that, unfortunately, Chuck's mom would lie for him when he was in trouble. Chuck was relieved. I was stuck. I was at an impasse.

I also knew it could make a difference in Chuck's future for him to be reprimanded for stealing something valuable—if he had taken the coat. And with that in the balance, it made the ethical choice for me, and I played my one and only remaining card.

I asked Chuck if he knew whether his coat, which I had folded in front of me on my desk, had an inside breast pocket. He answered yes. I offered him a deal. I told him that the boy who had reported the coat missing had placed his name on the inside of the breast pocket. My statement was totally fabricated, and that had been my ethical dilemma. But I was pretty sure that Chuck would not have looked in there. I told Chuck that if no name was inside that pocket, obviously everything would be fine and he could go back to class. If, however, I found the other boy's name was on the inside of the pocket, I would have to call his mother and suspend him for three days for stealing the coat.

Then I gave Chuck another option: if he told me the truth before we looked inside the pocket for the name, I would ask him to give the coat back to the boy, write a letter of apology, call his mother, and serve one day in the in-school suspension room.

Chuck sat for a few minutes, just thinking over his choices and then he asked me to repeat them. I did. He just sat in front of my desk looking up at the ceiling. Pretty soon I saw tears start to run down his cheeks. He just started talking spontaneously, explaining that he never had anything new and nice, and this coat was just so cool. He said that he took it in the fall from a locker that wasn't closed and put it in his backpack. He had waited until spring before wearing it to school, hoping that no one would be looking for it anymore.

Chuck was remorseful. He knew what he had done was wrong. I could also see how hard it was on him to let the thing go. I also knew he was going to be better for it. I told him that I was proud that he chose to tell the truth.

Having owned up, Chuck asked to look inside the pocket to see the name. I was sort of hoist by my own petard, then, and tried halfheartedly to sell him on the idea that didn't matter if there was or wasn't a name in the pocket—he had told the truth, and that's what mattered. That didn't fly: Chuck looked anyway, but, of course, there was no name. He shot me a look.

We called Chuck's mom, who started to make excuses for him, but quit quickly when I told the entire story. Chuck wrote a letter of apology while he spent the day in the suspension room. At the end of the day, in my office, Chuck gave the coat back to the original owner and told him he was sorry.

I couldn't possibly say there is any ethical absolute that could be formulated to fit all such situations. I only hope that all involved benefited from the greater truth that ultimately came out, and that my little white lie might get taken off the books.

Note from a high school parent:

Kevin informed us that he stayed home yesterday from school because he felt that his chemistry teacher would not understand why he didn't have his written report done on time. He used this time to complete the report. Please excuse Kevin and tell his teacher to accept his science paper.

THE STEWARDESS

The educator-to-be gets taught.

Before I became an educator I was, of course, being educated to be one. And did I ever learn some hard lessons.

Many things about college were great, especially the $25 one-way airline stand-by tickets that could be purchased by showing a college ID. At the college I attended, students were not allowed to have cars on campus during their first year, so my parents took me there in August, told me to fly home on the Wednesday prior to Thanksgiving, wished me luck, and left. That trip came quicker than seemed possible, and I wondered where the time could have gone as I found myself boarding a plane headed back to Chicago, back home for Thanksgiving.

The flight only lasted forty-five minutes, but those are forty-five minutes I'll never forget. The stewardess in the section of the plane where I was seated was about twenty years old and beautiful, with long, brunette hair pulled back in a ponytail. As she approached my row, I asked her if she flew out of Chicago. She smiled and said yes. I then asked her if she was home for the holidays and again she said yes. She then volunteered that she had to work on Thanksgiving Day and wouldn't get into Chicago until late Thursday evening but that she did not have to work on Friday.

I remember almost being unable to speak, but somehow I managed to ask her if she would like to go out on Friday evening. She asked me if I was home from college and where I lived. I told her, and she said that she would love to go out with me. My senses were reeling as though I'd been punched when she wrote her name and phone number on a piece of paper and handed it to me. Her name was Connie and she said that since she was getting in late on Thursday evening I could call her any time after 9:00 in the morning on Friday. I took the paper and asked her for another piece of paper so I could write down my name and phone number.

During the rest of the short flight, all I could think about was telling my friends that I had a date with a beautiful stewardess on Friday. I watched her work until we landed. She actually winked at me as I left the plane and said she was looking forward to hearing from me Friday morning. I can't remember touching the stairs going down to the tarmac. "This is so cool," I kept thinking. "This is just so cool."

My parents were waiting for me at O'Hare Airport, and I eagerly told my dad about how I had asked a stewardess to go on a date with me on Friday night and she had agreed! My dad was far more concerned about how I was doing in college, but at that moment I couldn't even think about my classes or grades. When we got home I immediately started calling all my friends and was wholeheartedly enjoying spreading my big news.

Thanksgiving Day was always a big event at our house with many guests. My sisters and I had to stay at home with our family until all the guests had left. As soon as the last person walked out the door, I called a couple of my friends to find out where everyone was hanging out that night, and then I headed to Joey's house. When I got there everyone was telling college freshman stories, which included their hardest classes, worst drunks, and new girlfriends. I felt so cool sharing news about my upcoming date with a stewardess. My friends sat in awe at my story. Any jealous disbelievers were silenced with a simple flash of the paper with her name and phone number in her own delicate hand.

When I got home I could hardly bring myself to go to bed and when I finally did I could hardly sleep. The anticipation was just too great.

At about 7:00 on Friday morning I came wide awake. I knew there was no point lying in bed, so I got up, cursing the thought that I had to wait two more hours before I could call Connie. After giving it a little more thought, though, I even decided to wait until 9:30 to call so I wouldn't appear too anxious.

I puttered away the hours with morning routine and lots of staring out windows.

By 9:05 I was a wreck, and all thought of waiting until 9:30 evaporated in an eye blink. I could not wait not a minute longer! I carefully took the piece of paper with Connie's number on it out of my wallet and quickly dialed. My heart was pounding as I waited for her to answer the phone.

One ring, two rings, finally it was picked up!

A soft female voice answered: "Good morning, Chicago Pest Control."

I held the phone away and stared at it, then almost died of embarrassment as I quickly hung it up. I grabbed the Yellow Pages and rapidly leafed through it to Pest Control and there it was—same number. I groaned.

There was no way I was going to tell my friends what had really happened. As the day wore on, I called as many of them as I could remember having told about my date and explained that Connie had been unexpectedly called to work a flight.

Since that day, my only conversations with flight attendants have been limited to a concise and direct response to their question, "What would you like to drink?"

Parent calling about a school delay:

"I just heard that school will be delayed two hours. Is that two hours from the start of the normal school day or two hours from the announcement on TV?"

MOTORCYCLE DISASTER

A young teacher playing good Samaritan quickly finds himself on the wrong road.

Ned Aldrich had just graduated from college and was excited to start his teaching career as our new seventh grade social studies teacher. Making the leap from a student in May to a teacher in September was easy for him. He was immediately accepted by the faculty and student body as a warm and friendly teacher. Ned was a sharp dresser and a handsome young man as well. The students also thought it was cool that he rode a motorcycle when the weather permitted. Ned coached seventh grade football and planned to coach basketball when that season arrived.

Ned's classroom management and teaching skills were very good for a first year teacher. Students knew what the expectations were and he worked hard to make sure that all his students were succeeding. After school he would stay to help kids who needed assistance and he even started a morning study session for those interested.

Many weekends for Ned were spent going back to his university to visit his girlfriend, who was a senior there. In October, about five weeks into the school year, Ned's girlfriend was free for the weekend and came to be with him. They attended a Friday night varsity home football game together. The middle school kids didn't know her and since he hadn't mentioned her, they were all very curious. So instead of having a lot of time to watch the game, Ned and his girlfriend spent most of the first quarter by the concession stand visiting with his students.

The following Monday morning at about 9:00 a.m., Melissa, a seventh grade student in Ned's class, went to the office of the counselor, Mrs. Becker, in tears and asked to speak to her. At the conclusion of her conversation with Melissa, Mrs. Becker explained to Melissa that she was going to have to go to the principal with this information. Melissa said she understood; the guidance office secretary was asked to sit in the room with Melissa while Mrs. Becker came to my office.

Mrs. Becket knocked at my open door and asked if she could meet with me privately. In our meeting, she gave me the following account by Melissa, referring to notes she had just taken in the interview with the girl:

On Saturday afternoon, Melissa—who lived about two blocks from Mr. Aldrich's apartment—was walking by just as he was leaving. He asked her if she had ever ridden on a motorcycle. She said no, and he invited her to take a short ride with him to the middle school where he was going to pick up some work to bring home. When they got to the middle school Melissa asked Mr. Aldrich when the new addition under construction would be completed. He told her about six months, but that if she wanted to see the part that was pretty much enclosed they could explore it before going to his classroom.

When they got inside the enclosed construction area, Melissa said that Mr. Aldrich gave her a hug, took down his pants, and asked her to touch him, which she said she did. They then went to his classroom to get his work and he took her home.

When Mrs. Becker finished reading the account that Melissa had given her, I asked her what she thought. Mrs. Becker said that Melissa told her the story three times and each account was the same with only a few minor added or deleted comments. In her twenty years as a school counselor, she had heard kids give similar accounts and felt that Melissa's story seemed credible.

Mrs. Becker went back to the guidance office to be with Melissa. I called Ned into my office and sent a paraprofessional into his classroom to watch the kids. I asked him if he had given Melissa a ride on his motorcycle Saturday afternoon and he said, "Yes." I asked him if he had taken her to the middle school and showed her the new construction site and he said, "Yes." I asked him if he had taken her to his classroom to get work and then had taken her home and he said, "Yes." Then I told him what Melissa claimed to have happened at the construction site. He went pale. He was completely shocked, instantly denying her story.

I explained carefully to Ned that I needed him to write down exactly what had happened Saturday. I also told him bluntly that he had used very poor judgment by giving her a ride on his motorcycle, taking her to the construction site, and being alone with her. He understood and he agreed. Melissa seemed lonely at school, didn't have a lot of friends, and had confided in him about her parents going through a divorce that summer; he felt sorry for her. He never even thought about the possibility of her fabricating such a story or accusing him of something so terrible.

As a young administrator, I needed assistance with this issue and asked the high school principal to meet with me to discuss the next steps. This was 1975 and the processes we have today for this type of situation simply did not exist. While Ned went off to write his account, the high school principal helped me write out a series of steps to follow in conducting an investigation.

My next step was to call Melissa's mother and ask her to come to school. Mrs. Becker and I explained the entire situation to her. Melissa's mother was a caring and concerned parent and admitted that Melissa had gone through a very difficult summer and had been acting like a different person. She had entered puberty, her father had moved out of the house, and her best friend had moved out of state. All of these changes had left her an emotional mess. Melissa had revealed that her favorite teacher was Mr. Aldrich and that he made her feel important again, as well as really helping her with social studies.

Mrs. Becker and Melissa's mother then left my office together to talk to Melissa—the next step on my written plan.

Soon Ned returned with his written account of the incident. We reviewed it, and it was identical to what he had told me earlier. Ned asked me a pointed question: "If this is her word against mine and she stays with her story, I'm finished as a teacher forever, aren't I?" I explained to him that Melissa's mother, Mrs. Becker and Melissa were talking. For now, all he could do was sit tight and wait.

I knew very well, though, that this incident had the potential of causing Ned serious problems as a teacher. He had placed himself in a situation with Melissa that had all the explosive components for serious consequences.

By 2:00 p.m. Mrs. Becker and Melissa's mother decided that Melissa would go home with her mom. Melissa's mom wanted some time alone with her daughter to talk to her about the alleged incident. Melissa's mom remarked privately to us that she questioned the accuracy of Melissa's story because she believed that Melissa would have told her about what happened before she would have come to school and told Mrs. Becker.

During the rest of the afternoon and into the evening, Melissa did not change her story. She just cried a lot. Later that evening, Melissa's mother called Mrs. Becker to ask if she and Melissa could come in the next morning so all three of them could talk some more. That was arranged. They arrived at 8:00 a.m. the next day and went straight to the guidance office.

Knowing that Melissa had not yet changed her story, Ned was very concerned as he walked down the hallway to teach his first hour class. Mrs. Becker and I had decided that if Melissa had not changed her story by noon we would have to contact the school attorney. This was rolling down the road toward big trouble.

At 11:15 a.m. Mrs. Becker came to my office and asked if she could arrange for Ned to come to the guidance office to meet with Melissa and her mom. Melissa had something to say but she would not tell anyone unless Mr. Aldrich was present. I wasted no time at all in summoning Mr. Aldrich from his classroom. We went to the guidance office together. Whatever this was going to be, good or bad, I wanted to be there.

Melissa was in tears. None of us was at ease, but all tried to make it as easy as possible. Through her tears, and sometimes sobs, Melissa explained that she saw Mr. Aldrich with his girlfriend at the Friday night football game and that it broke her heart because she had a huge crush on him. She had felt sure that he felt the same way about her. When she saw him Saturday morning leaving his apartment and he asked her if she wanted a ride on his motorcycle, she was excited. When she held on to him as they rode, she felt wonderful. He just showed her the construction site, got his work from his classroom, and then took her home. She was crushed and became very jealous of Mr. Aldrich's girlfriend. She decided to hurt him by making up a story that she knew would get him in trouble.

Mrs. Becker explained to Melissa that sometimes people make very serious mistakes and that these mistakes can hurt others for the rest of their lives. If someone has the opportunity to correct a mistake before it causes permanent damage, then often times things can change back to the way they were. Melissa tearfully pleaded that she wanted Mr. Aldrich to be her friend even though she had lied and tried to get him in trouble.

We decided that Melissa needed to be with her mom for the rest of the day. Later that afternoon Melissa's mom called and said she felt it would be best for Melissa to have a different social studies teacher, which was easily arranged.

Ned, of course, was immensely relieved. We meticulously documented the whole incident so in the future if anyone questioned what had happened, there was a formal accounting of everything. In the write-up there was a clause warning Ned that he should never give students rides on his motorcycle or in his car. This was a serious mistake on his part and, while well intended, he used very poor judgment which could have cost him his teaching license. Ned is still teaching today and considered an outstanding social studies teacher.

Melissa did not tell this story to anyone again. She finished middle school and did quite well in high school. Mrs. Becker had done a wonderful job of working with Melissa and her mother, which actually helped save Mr. Aldrich's job. Melissa's mother deserved much of the credit; she understood her daughter well enough to spend time with her and keep talking about the situation instead of making a formal accusation and going to the police.

When I tell this story to aspiring teachers as they start their practicum, they always squirm in their seats. It could happen to any teacher. A number of young teachers have told me later that they had subsequently found themselves in a situation where they could have given a student a ride somewhere, but having heard this story they simply insisted on finding another way to transport the student.

☏ Call from an upset coach:

"I coach for the district and want to know if I can have practice this afternoon even though school has been cancelled." The secretary responded by saying that a decision regarding practice would be made later in the day and would depend on the weather and the plowing schedule at the high school. The coach replied, "I don't care if the parking lots are clean, I just want to get into the gym."

VALENTINE'S "GIFT"

*A card that is a prank—something
everyone can give!*

The practical joke, the prank, will never die as an art form as long as there are educational institutions. Apparently no learning can occur in any form without the periodic assistance of slapstick and ridiculous tricks being played in all directions.

Our Director of Attendance and Transportation, Curt, was a knave in the pranks department and a past master at the craft. I had been on the receiving end of his chicanery more than once. So in my second year as superintendent in the district, just prior to Valentine's Day, I decided on the inarguable basis of complete whim that it was about time for somebody to turn the tables and have a little good-natured fun with Curt.

To that lofty end, I raided local stores and bought a box of 2,000 BBs, a large bag of M&Ms, a pipe cleaner, a medium-sized styrofoam coffee cup, a stiff but thin piece of cardboard on which to set the cup, and a nice Valentine's Day Card from a secretary to her boss. I was all set.

In the clandestine sanctity of my office on Valentine's Day, I cut out the bottom of the coffee cup. I then bent the pipe cleaner into a curve and punched each end through the sides of the coffee cup, near the top, so it formed a handle for the "basket." I placed the cup on the piece of cardboard, then filled the cup about two-thirds full of BBs. As the finishing touch, I poured M&M's on top of the BBs to fill the remainder of the cup to the top, and enjoyed a nice, wicked grin. The card is probably the most important part. It's the bait. I wrote a warm note from Curt's secretary on the inside thanking him for making the workplace a fun place to be and for being a good supervisor. I enjoyed an even more wicked smile.

When I knew the coast was clear, I carefully steadied the cup on the stiff cardboard, carried it to Curt's office, and set it directly in the center of his desk. Applying a little pressure on the top of the cup, I slid the cardboard out so that the bottom of the cup was now resting directly on his desk. I leaned the Valentine's card against the cup and its pipe cleaner handle. Aw, it looked sweet!

I couldn't be there to watch, but I had cleared it all with his secretary, who later delivered the following account to me:

Curt came into the office at about 8:30 a.m. after making sure all the buses had safely returned from their morning routes. He took off his coat, walked over to his desk, saw his gift, and smiled. He opened the card. After reading the nice note inside, he seemed a little embarrassed when he thanked his secretary for the thoughtful gift. Before she could respond, he asked if she'd like some of the M&Ms and lifted the cup toward her, then jumped back with a little "Oh!" as 2,000 BBs bounced and rolled toward every point of the compass across his glass-covered desktop and cascaded to the floor.

She tittered as he stared, then they both burst out laughing.

Curt tried to pry out of her who had delivered his "present," since he knew perfectly well it wasn't her doing. Even though she pretended to know nothing, Curt quickly figured out that I was the culprit. He still finds an occasional BB in his desk drawer!

All right, fun's over, back to class. And any of you school-age kids reading this are to take with you the moral of this story, which clearly is that practical jokes aren't funny. Only be serious in your studies. That's what prepares you for life. Now put this down and go do your homework!

Note from a middle school parent :

Please excuse Jimmy from school yesterday. He was sick, but his two friends played outside in our backyard most of the day, so call me and I'll tell you their names in case they called in sick, too!

CITY BOY HAYSEED

A stranger in a strange land learns that the tables can turn—real quick-like.

Though I grew up in the Chicago suburbs and worked part-time jobs downtown, the college I attended was in a small town twelve miles outside a Midwestern metropolitian area. That experience was one of the best things that happened to me. I finally took education more seriously, met and married my wife, and we both started our first jobs teaching vocal and instrumental music in the rural school system of that same small community where the college was located.

The kindergarten through twelfth grade enrollment in this school system was 225. There were about twenty students in each grade level. The school building, which sat atop a hill overlooking the small business section of town, housed all the grades. The superintendent was also the elementary school principal; the high school principal was also the junior high school principal; the custodian was also the bus driver.

On the first day at the faculty meeting, the superintendent walked around the room expressing his excitement over the number of returning teachers and welcoming the new teachers like my wife and me. It was typical for young, new teachers like us to get their first teaching jobs in small rural schools and then move on to a larger school district after gaining a few years of experience.

The superintendent/elementary principal segued from welcoming warmth to the all-business briefing. While looking pointedly at me, he explained that it was unacceptable for male teachers to have hair over their collars and tops of their ears or sideburns lower than their ear lobes. I smiled pleasantly, mentally planning a stop at the barbershop. At least I wasn't the only hirsute new male teacher—which provided but little comfort under his penetrating gaze.

Continuing with the expectations for all faculty members, he explained that while it was tempting to be friends with high school students, it was critical that young new teachers make the break from being a student to being a teacher. "Kids want you to be friendly, not friends," he said and then went on to tell us not to be too friendly until about November. "It is easier to relax a little than it is to try and get tough after you have lost your edge," he stressed. He then told us he always could tell who was doing a good job with discipline by looking at which teachers' names were written on the bathroom stalls by the students.

Following the meeting, the new art teacher and I joked in the hall about having to go to the barbershop after school and about the teachers' names on the stall walls. While chatting, we hit upon what we knew just had to be a brilliant and original idea: we decided to get an edge on impressing the superintendent by writing our own names on the bathroom walls.

On the second day of school the new art teacher and I were called into the superintendent's office. On his desk there was an aerosol solvent can and two rags. "If you guys had waited a month," he said, "I might have believed that you didn't write your own names on the walls. It's way too early for the kids to start writing, but it's not too late for you to go clean yours off the walls. And don't try it again." As we were leaving, he complimented us on our new haircuts. Quite embarrassed, we went directly to the restroom to clean our names off the walls.

At the time I was driving a 1969 Plymouth Road Runner, canary yellow with a black hood and a dark green vinyl roof. It had a 383 engine with a four-barrel carburetor. Instead of a honking noise, the horn made a "beep-beep" sound just like the cartoon character. On the third day after school, some of the high school kids wanted to drag race, and it was then that I realized the importance of the superintendent's message about the difference between being friends with students versus being friendly. So I just said "no thanks" and added that I didn't want to embarrass any of them if they lost—and they probably would have lost. Pity I couldn't prove it. This made a few of the seniors with hot cars really upset and from then on they were always giving me static about my crummy Plymouth with a funny horn.

The school year was underway, and my wife and I were commuting about eighty miles a day. That got old very fast. A hog farmer in the local community who had just finished building a new home about three hundred yards from his old farmhouse knew about our long commute and asked me if we would like to rent the older home from him for $80 a month. At the time we were paying $150 and had college loans to pay, so we leapt at his offer. He also let me park my car in one side of the old two-car garage. The other side of the garage housed oil and grease barrels with long hoses that allowed the old boy to drive his tractor up close and add oil and grease when needed.

Shortly after we moved into the farmhouse, I started noticing there were little black specks on the yellow paint and the green top of my Road Runner. I also noticed that there were flies all over the place and some dead ones on the barrels. I decided that the flies must be landing on top of the barrels, getting oil and grease on their wings and legs, then transferring it to my car. To try to stop it, I first cleaned the tops of the barrels off, then cleaned the specks off my car and figured all was fine.

The next day my car had specks on it again. I decided to ask around and find out if anybody knew what might be causing it.

The superintendent's secretary was married to the vocational agriculture teacher, so I figured she would be pretty knowledgeable about flies and other rural mysteries. I told her what had happened and what I had done. When I got to the part about cleaning the oil barrels, the woman started laughing so hard that she had tears in her eyes. She called her husband's classroom and asked him to come to the office. Meanwhile, the superintendent had come to the office to see what all the commotion was. I stood with my face screwed up in a confused frown.

Once her impromptu audience had gathered, she asked me to repeat my story. I began to suspect that perhaps there was a flaw in it somewhere. By the time I finished, all three of them were laughing hysterically. They explained to me that the black specks left by the flies had nothing to do with the oil barrels—it was fly dung!

The story circulated throughout the school and small community in less than two days. My only salvation was that I was a city kid, so they cut me a little slack. I don't think I ever got hung with the title "Lord of the Flies." If I did, I never heard about it.

That following week, though, when I saw the farmer on his tractor stopped by the hog lots, I walked over and greeted him. He just started laughing and said he had wondered who cleaned the tops of his barrels and why. When he had heard the story at the feed store about the flies, he was laughing so hard he could barely drive home. I just smiled and laughed along with him. In an attempt to redeem myself and be amiable, I decided to start a conversation with him about his hog operation. "So, how many Black Angus hogs do you have at any one time?" I asked.

He almost fell off his tractor, he laughed so hard. After gaining his composure, he climbed down from the tractor, walked me over to the fifty head of cattle he had next to the hog lot and said, "These are Black Angus cattle, son. My hogs are Hampshire." As he climbed back onto his tractor, he was still laughing and shaking his head.

The next Monday when I arrived at school, a bulletin board showcased a photo of the head of a hog pasted on a photo of the body of a cow and inscribed with the words, "Black Angus Hogs—only in Chicago." That joke haunted me wherever I went for weeks stretching into months. They have long memories in those close-knit rural communities. First grade students even snickered about it. I have to say, though, that it was never a mean-spirited ribbing. They always somehow made me feel like I was just earning my stripes among them.

Then I found out what earning my stripes really entailed. During that same year, the band uniforms, numbering fifty, needed replacing at a cost of $125 for each uniform. One of the fundraiser events held to raise the money to purchase the new uniforms was a band-sponsored auction. Each volunteer would be "auctioned off" to work for the highest bidder for either a half or full day following the 7:00 a.m. auction. The auction was a big deal in the small community and was well attended. The music boosters even served breakfast. I volunteered to be on the auction block though I was a little leery about who might bid on me and what work I would be doing. As it turned out, two farmers with kids in the band pooled their resources and bid $250 for me. "Oh good," I thought, "two uniforms for one day's work!"

For my chore, they each had a chicken coop that needed cleaning. "That's not so bad," I thought to myself. After the auction I followed them to the first farm and they told me I would have to change clothes and wear a mask. At this point I figured they were just kidding around until they handed me coveralls, rubber boots, and a mask resembling a surgical mask. Not knowing anything about chicken coops, I changed clothes, put the mask on top of my head and headed for the coop with a scoop shovel. They explained my job and told me to come back to the barn when I was finished.

The smell was simply unbelievable.

I had never smelled a stronger ammonia odor in my life. Even with the mask on, my eyes began to water to the point where I could hardly see and my nose ran like a faucet. Each time I filled the shovel, it seemed as though the smell worsened—which was not possible.

After about thirty minutes, my perceptions swimming in a sea of ammonia, I became dimly aware that the farmers were at the opening to the coop. They had decided they better come to rescue me since I hadn't demonstrated enough sense to come out for air. They steadied me and directed me to the barn where I could shower and change back into my clothes.

Once I was fit for human company again, they invited me to stay for lunch and I spent the afternoon listening to them tell mesmerizing stories about this amazing little town.

The fact that I cleaned out chicken coops for band uniforms was a hit in the community. The kids, of course, absolutely gagged when I told them about my chore. I omitted the fact that I only did it for thirty minutes. I had achieved at least minor hero status and wasn't about to compromise it. We raised $3,750 dollars that Saturday and soon had enough to place the order with the uniform company, the balance being raised through generous donations, a lot of bake sales and wild game suppers.

The two years I spent in that rural setting were educational beyond anything I had ever learned in college. It helped me, a city kid, understand that a culture I had once viewed as almost backwards was anything but. The folks and kids in this community were down-to-earth, caring, hard-working, and wise beyond words. They were always willing to offer a helping hand to someone in need. They knew the value of education and their kids worked hard in school. To this day I still have contact with some of the folks I knew from this great community.

This is one city kid who learned more from the country folks than he could ever possibly return.

Note from a middle school parent:

Shannon missed school yesterday because his friend who skipped school came over to play after I left for work.

SMOKE FROM THE COLLAR

Smoking Wars Part II: Is your shirt on fire, or are you just unhappy to see me?

George was one of the most creative and elusive smokers in the student body and was also among the nicest and most likeable of the bunch. But one day his luck ran out.

The smarter students knew that the key to not getting caught smoking in the restroom was having a good lookout system. This system required at least one person in the group who either was a nonsmoker or who was not going to smoke at that time. This person's role would be to wait just outside the bathroom door or be stationed just inside the door. In either positioning, he could say hello loudly to the teacher or supervisor as they approached the door or entered the restroom. Then everyone in the restroom who was smoking would flip their cigarettes into the toilet or urinal, causing a quick sequence of hissing sounds as the glowing end of the cigarette hit the water, followed by a volley of flushing.

One day George got sloppy or overly cocky and happened to be smoking in the restroom without a lookout. Unfortunately for him, I was on the prowl.

Recently I had asked the janitor to oil the hinges of the restroom doors so they didn't squeak as they opened or shut. I also was wearing rubber soled shoes, so I was Mr. Stealth as I roamed the not-so-hallowed halls.

I came to the boys' restroom and paused for a moment outside. I could smell the cigarette smoke through the door. That didn't always mean that someone was smoking at that moment, but I swung the door silently open to find out.

As I entered the restroom, George was standing in the center of the room, but no cigarette was apparent. Smoke hung in the air. I said, "Hello George, how's it going?" He didn't respond right away. He was wearing a green army coat that was knee length and too long for his arms so his hands were hidden. I looked around but I didn't see a cigarette anywhere on the floor nor had I heard the telltale hissing sound as I had silently entered the room. But George didn't look terribly happy.

Rather quickly, George said, "Well, I suppose I should be getting to class." George held the school record for tardies to class so his new concern about being on time was interesting. Besides, the bell hadn't even sounded yet to end the lunch period. And I was between him and the door. I gave no ground. I asked him point blank: "George, was there someone in here previously who was smoking or were you smoking?"

George shrugged. He said he hadn't seen anybody when he came in, but then assured me that he, of course, would never smoke in the restroom since it was against school rules. It was about then that I noticed gray-blue tendrils of smoke wafting from George's collar where his coat rested against his neck. Maybe the shrug is what did it.

"George," I said, "I see smoke starting to come out from under your coat by your neck. I feel sure that you don't want to burn your hand or catch your coat on fire, so why don't you just put it out and we can go to the office."

At that, George smiled guiltily and stretched his arms so his hands came out of the sleeves, flipped the cigarette into the nearest toilet, flushed it, and admitted, "I thought if I just waited you out I would have gotten by again. This has worked so many times with other folks. Crap, my dad is going to kill me."

George and I walked to the office so he could explain to the high school vice-principal what had happened. He demonstrated his "now you see it, now you don't" sleight of hand technique of cupping the cigarette and drawing it up into his coat.

We all had to laugh. George called his dad to come and get him from school, the usual penalties were levied, and the incident forgotten.

Two years later when George graduated, he stopped by my house and gave me a gift certificate to his dad's store. His dad owned and operated a very fine cigar and tobacco store in a major mall. He told me that he had smoked a cigarette every day during the noon hour for three years and had fooled everyone but me. I was the only person who ever actually caught him smoking in school.

He then volunteered some tips for catching student smokers in the future that I would never have thought of. Sorry, but they are my secret now.

Call from a parent:

"As a parent, I just want you to know that I completely disagree with the decision to have school today when others are not. I know we didn't get much snow, but those schools fifteen miles south of us have cancelled school and it's not fair."

CAUGHT AND RELEASED

Bad judgment allows a teacher to get
away with crossing a bright red line.

Mr. Neal, a young high school math teacher, was very popular with the students. He was a sharp-looking guy who stood six feet two inches tall, and he had dark hair, sunken eyes, and a radiant personality.

When young, new teachers start at the high school level, it is critical that they distance themselves from high school students who want to be their friends—or more. That isn't uncommon, since there often is only a four-year age difference between a high school senior and a first year teacher. To help new teachers understand the importance of this distinction, part of the in-service training for new teachers focuses on "being friendly" versus "being friends" with students. These are two completely separate things and knowing the difference is crucial.

As the middle school principal, I wasn't directly involved with Mr. Neal, who was teaching in the high school. The high school principal, Mr. Daniels, expressed some concerns to me one day that Mr. Neal was having problems making the distinction between "being friends" and "being friendly." He asked me to keep an eye on Mr. Neal when we shared gym supervision time.

After lunch, students could go into the high school gym to visit with friends, run around, and shoot hoops. The high school kids were on one end of the gym and the middle school kids on the other end. A high school teacher supervised the gym area while I monitored the lunchroom area, but since there were up to 150 kids, I often wandered to the gym to help.

Mr. Daniels advised me to watch for any out-of-the-ordinary conduct. I enjoyed Mr. Neal's company and didn't notice anything unusual, so the request diminished in importance over time.

Then one day about a month later, I was walking through the gym on my way to the lunchroom. The gym was empty because the students were still at lunch, but I heard quiet laughter coming from the balcony behind the bleachers. The balcony housed gymnastics and was off limits, though I sometimes had to chase kids out of there after lunch. In my rubber-soled shoes, I decided to investigate.

As I neared the top I was surprised to recognize the voice of Mr. Neal, then heard the voice of a female. With the next step or two, my head came just above the balcony floor through the stair opening. I saw a senior girl, Brenda, sitting on the vaulting horse with Mr. Neal standing in front of her. They were speaking in tones too low to hear clearly. She laughed at something he said—and they kissed. Then they kissed again.

Not knowing what to do, I quietly stepped back down the stairs and went to supervise the lunchroom. I was a young administrator just twenty-eight years old at the time. I had already made my first serious mistake with this situation.

When the lunch period ended, I went straight to Mr. Daniels and told him what I had witnessed between Mr. Neal and Brenda. He rather urgently asked if I had made my presence known to them. I said I hadn't. I quickly got a firm, even stern, mentoring lesson on what now would be a potential "I said/he said" situation. Mr. Daniels grimly asked me to document in writing the entire incident and sign it so he at least had an official account to present to Mr. Neal when he confronted him with the allegation.

After I wrote out the incident, I headed back to the middle school, kicking myself for not having thought to reveal myself to the pair in the balcony so that they couldn't deny my discovery. Mr. Daniels asked me to return at the end of the day for a meeting of all involved.

The two and a half hours between the time I left Mr. Daniels's office and the end of school crept by. I was very nervous about the entire situation and wished I were present during the initial meetings. But Mr. Daniels said he knew Brenda and her family well and he thought it best to visit with her alone. After his meeting with Brenda, he would meet with Mr. Neal.

After dwelling on the situation for over two hours, I had that awful "terror stomach" on my way to Mr. Daniels office. I reflected that it might be how kids felt who had to come and see me.

Mr. Daniels reported that Brenda admitted talking to Mr. Neal on the balcony about some problems she was having with her friends, but she said she would never kiss him, as she knew he was married. Mr. Neal confessed to being with Brenda on the balcony, but he also said that they were talking about issues she was having with her friends. He was adamant that he would never kiss her or any student, and he demanded to know why I would fabricate such a story. He also questioned why, if I really had seen something, I didn't say anything to him or Brenda at the time.

I think I sunk deeper into my chair as I listened. We had another meeting with Mr. Neal. By this time my stomach felt like it was no longer part of my body and I was very cold. Mr. Daniels asked me to repeat my story to Mr. Neal. He asked Mr. Neal not to interrupt or make any comments until I was done talking. After I finished my account of the incident, Mr. Neal became very upset and started making threats and accusing me of fabricating the story. He said I was trying to ruin his teaching career and his marriage. He was quite agitated and, at one point, stood up and asked me to step outside to settle this.

Being a seasoned administrator, Mr. Daniels quickly calmed the situation by telling Mr. Neal that there would be no formal discipline or sanctions, since it was basically my word against Mr. Neal's and Brenda's.

Then Mr. Daniels fixed Mr. Neal with a stare over his glasses and said, "But I am very disappointed with you for being alone with a female student on the balcony at all, at any time, under any circumstances, much less when you were supposed to have been on duty in the gym— all of which you have admitted to. And if there ever is even one more incident where you are found alone with any female student discussing her social problems, you *will* receive a written reprimand, and since you are a probationary teacher, you can be recommended for contract non-renewal. Have I left any room for misinterpretation?"

I could have cheered.

Mr. Neal admitted using poor judgment and promised that it wouldn't happen again.

After Mr. Neal left, Mr. Daniels and I talked for another hour about the entire situation, start to finish. When you witness such a situation, he pointed out, it is imperative to go directly to the people involved at the time and ask them to accompany you to the office right away. This way there is no doubt that they know what you have seen and there also is no opportunity for them to discuss their stories prior to an interview. Mr. Daniels believed that Brenda, who was facing towards me as she sat on the vaulting horse on the balcony, probably got a glimpse of me as I withdrew down the stairs. They both then coordinated their stories. Mr. Daniels said he believed they collaborated because normally both parties would just deny they were there together unless they knew someone had seen them.

After that incident Mr. Neal said very little to me and made very little eye contact with me. He never made any more threats or expressed any anger. At no time in the future did he get into any similar situations. He continued to be a very popular high school teacher and eventually finished his master's degree in administration. He left the state and went into administration as a principal and later became an area administrator.

Jeff missed the music contest on Saturday because he was too sick to play his trumpet. While we know there wasn't school Saturday, his band teacher will probably lower his grade for missing the event and we don't think that is fair since he was sick. We returned late Sunday evening from our weekend in Chicago.

WHITEOUT WEEKEND. . .

*. . .strands the jazz band's
unplanned caravan.*

One story in every veteran educator's repertoire is the tale of having to stay overnight with school kids on a trip because of a storm that paralyzes all transportation. These tales reach urban legend status. Until I was in my twenty-fifth year in education and a superintendent, these were just stories to me—thankfully I had not experienced any such situation first hand. Some greater power, though, apparently felt I had been deprived somehow, and set out to correct that oversight in March of that year.

One of the universities in our state annually hosted a large jazz band competition in early March. Only the top high school jazz bands entered this event and the competition was keen. Bands that placed first or second moved on to a larger, statewide competition.

The easy, two-hour Saturday morning drive to the university contest was always one of the highlights of the year for our school's jazz band. They had won this competition previously and were always among the favorites at the festival. This particular year, although I was superintendent of schools, my wife and I made the trip simply as proud parents of one of the jazz band members. Parents of the musicians for all the bands congregated at the University Theater, where the judging was done, to listen and cheer after each performance.

The performances by all these young musicians from various schools were simply outstanding that day. In the late afternoon a ceremony was held to present some of the awards and end the day program, but the evening concert performance was where the remaining top contenders did their best numbers for final judging and awards.

It was an exciting evening. Each jazz band was excellent and none of us envied the judges in having to select a first place winner. In the end, to our joy and surprise, our band had been awarded first place!

All the parents of our jazz band students were excited, and my wife and I felt honored to be among them. Everyone agreed spontaneously to form a caravan behind the bus and make the two-hour drive home together in celebration of this wonderful evening.

As we gathered the music equipment to help load it into the band bus, the driver mentioned that there were weather reports of light to moderate snowfall in the area, but she didn't seem too concerned. There was no snow falling where we were. Some parents called friends in our town to check if there was any snow there and were told that everything was clear. I called the weather service that the district subscribed to and was informed that snow was forming, but it didn't look heavy.

Just in case any weather problems did develop, we decided to take a route that went through a town about every twenty miles. That way we would always be near help in case we needed assistance.

As we pulled out of the university complex, the bus driver led the way headed south toward our town. We were about ten miles into the trip on the two-lane state highway when we encountered the first snow. And it was heavy, blowing snow, not light flurries. I was behind the bus and could see only about fifty feet in any direction. There were twelve other cars in our caravan behind my van. My wiper blades were keeping up with the snowfall and, while the road surface was getting snow packed, it was still very passable. We had slowed from the fifty-five mile per hour speed limit to about thirty miles per hour when the bus driver pulled over to the side of the road and stopped, turning on the emergency flashers.

I followed suit and the caravan followed me. I got out of the van and pulled my collar up, trotting along the crunching, snow-covered shoulder of the road up to the bus entry door to see what the problem was. The windshield wipers on the bus were having trouble keeping up with the snowfall; ice was forming on them as the snow melted on the windshield and refroze. The bus driver cleaned the wipers and asked if I would drive my van in front of the bus. She would feel more at ease if she could follow someone instead of leading the way with that big bus.

While we were stopped, the snow had intensified and the radio now was warning drivers that an unpredicted snowstorm had formed over this part of the state and was causing whiteouts in some places due to the high winds and heaviness of the snowfall. Travel was not recommended.

I had heard of whiteouts but had never experienced anything like we were about to encounter. We were driving in at least somewhat passable conditions when in an instant my depth perception was almost completely erased. The only thing visible in front of the windshield was the color white. It reminded me of holding your hand right in front of your eyes, except it was bright white instead of flesh color. I could not see the front end of my van. I had slowed to between five and ten miles per hour, and we still had nearly six miles to go before we arrived at the next town.

Friends who were riding in the car with us suggested that it might help to roll down the driver's window to look sideways at the road. Looking out the side window did help some, so we rolled down the passenger side as well and kept watch in both directions to navigate. We could see dim ghosts of rural mailboxes on each side as we passed them. Sometimes the mailboxes were very close to the passenger side and sometimes very close to the driver's side, which was alarming since that meant at times we were on the wrong side of the road! We were very thankful that we weren't meeting any oncoming traffic during this treacherous, harrowing forty-five minutes.

As we reached the outskirts of the next town, we could faintly see a sign for a gas station and convenience store. With a slumping relief, I headed gingerly into the station and the caravan crept in behind me. At almost the same time as we arrived, two fire engines turned into the station from the other direction and pulled up to the gas pumps, surreal looking red behemoths rolling slowly to a stop against a swirling gray-white background of wind-whipped snow.

We learned that the firefighters had just returned from attempting to put out a fire at a farm home. Unfortunately, the fire could not be controlled and the home had been lost.

The fire chief told us that the storm was supposed to continue for the next two hours and drop about a foot of blowing and drifting snow. This was awful news. The chief could see our plight, with carloads of parents and a bus full of band students, and suggested we follow them to the fire station, about two blocks away, where we could stay the night in their meeting room. He said it was big enough to easily house our group.

With untold and untellable relief and gratitude, we followed the engines to the fire station and unloaded what we had that might make the night passable. It was a great comfort to be in a warm, dry, safe place, protected from the miserable and dangerous conditions we had been caught in. The firefighters who lived in town called their wives and they brought blankets and pillows for all of us. They made sure that students whose parents were not with our group called home to tell their parents we were all safe.

I carried a blank school check with me in case of an emergency, and it seemed to me that this certainly qualified, so we ordered pizza from the local restaurant for all the kids and parents. The local movie theater, one block from the fire station, was showing *Home Alone 2* and, even though it was closed, the people who ran the theater invited us to come down anyway. They ran the movie free of charge.

By the time the moviegoers returned at about 1:30 a.m., the snow had stopped. There were drifts everywhere, some as tall as ten feet. The kids, who were pretty excited with the adventures of the evening, were ready to stay up all night and talk. The parents, on the other hand, were ready to sleep! A compromise was reached at about 3:00 a.m. and everyone found places on the floor to attempt to get some sleep. The sounds that filled the fire station in those wee hours were a mixture of kids laughing and making funny noises and parents snoring loudly, which caused the kids to laugh even more. This continued until daybreak. Those of us who stayed awake had fun just listening to all of it.

By mid-morning most of the major roads were plowed and now just wet with large snow banks on either side serving as ghostly reminders of what we had faced the night before. The temperature, which had risen to about forty-five degrees, was causing the snow to melt quickly. With long-winded thanks to our kind firefighter hosts, we loaded the caravan up and were able to get on the road without incident. By the time we got back to our town, there was no snow at all. The storm had only covered the northern part of the state. After all of the music equipment was unloaded at school, everyone went home to rest.

To show appreciation for the kindness shown to us by the firefighters, the band students, along with their parents, raised quite a bit of money through donations for a new "jaws of life" tool that the fire department had been saving money to purchase. They sent us a wonderful article from their local paper as a thank you for our donation.

So now, after an unexpected March snowstorm, I can play the role of the wise elder telling young teachers and administrators about the horrors of a whiteout blizzard, getting snowed in, and spending the night with kids. It is no longer a myth—it is unassailable fact.

A month later, the jazz band won the state championship.

Note from an elementary school parent:

Barb was absent for the past three days due to the flu. She threw up the first day, had diarrhea the second day, and was still dehydrated yesterday. We felt that since she spent so much time in the bathroom the first two days, she needed the rest yesterday.

HEADED FOR THE CORNFIELD

It's hard to help some find direction in life.

It was October and the school year was well underway. I was the middle school principal and in my second year as an administrator. A new family moved into the school district over one weekend, and the new student, Jason, and his mother, Sherry, came to my office on the following Tuesday to register him for school.

Jason was a small boy with scraggly blonde hair that needed both washing and cutting. His clothes were clean but wrinkled. Jason's mom confided in me that her son did have some trouble concentrating in class and had been in some minor trouble at his previous school, but she assured me that it had been nothing too serious. She explained that they had moved quite a lot due to her husband's job in the construction business, which was driving large tractors for earth-moving companies.

After providing the district with the address and phone number of his previous school and completing the necessary paperwork to request Jason's records, she asked if he could start school that day. We told her he was welcome to start and we would assign another student as his mentor. Sherry paid his fees and lunch money for the rest of the week and left.

Mrs. Jamison, the school counselor, was called to my office to be introduced to Jason so she could help set up his schedule, get his books, and assign him a mentor. Soon Jason and his mentor went off to class. When Mrs. Jamison came back to my office, she commented that Jason was very quiet, never made eye contact with her or his assigned mentor, and really didn't communicate much of anything to her, which was unusual. Being slightly concerned, she decided to make another contact with Jason after lunch.

By lunchtime, Jason's mentor had come to the office and said he wanted to be removed from being the boy's mentor since Jason had been making fun of him for being a mentor. He said that Jason had called him a "wuss" and told him that he didn't need his help. I asked Mrs. Jamison to find Jason and talk to him. When she tried talking to Jason, he told her to leave him alone. "I don't need your help; I'll be just fine," he said.

A call to Jason's previous school revealed that while he had only been there for two months, he had been referred to the office numerous times for inappropriate behavior with other kids as well as repeatedly being late to class. They had never received any records from his previous school. While he had never caused any physical harm to anyone, he was described as being moody and a loner. He called kids names, wrote nasty notes, and made sexual comments to girls. They explained that they had never met his father and that his mother didn't seem to be able to do much about controlling him.

During the last period of the day I called Jason into my office to ask him how his first day had gone. He said he thought the other kids were really immature, he didn't like his teachers, and he didn't want to be at school. In answer to my question, "What do you like most about school?" he responded, "Nothing!" That pretty much summed up his entire outlook on school: he knew it was the law that he had to attend school, otherwise he wouldn't be bothering. So much for day one, I thought.

Mrs. Jamison asked Jason's teachers to stop by her office after school to share their opinions of his first day. Their reports were pretty consistent: he was very quiet, and although he was not disruptive in class he made no effort to participate or even open a book; he just stared out the window. Mrs. Jamison asked if I would call Jason's mother and ask her to come to school the next day for a conference. Sherry agreed to bring Jason to school the next morning and meet with us at 8:00 a.m.

The next morning Mrs. Jamison, Sherry, and I met to discuss Jason's first day and to ask her to share any information about Jason that could help us make the rest of his seventh grade year more productive. Sherry said that Jason had never liked school and had been in a special class two schools ago for kids who were emotionally disturbed, but that she had refused to allow him to continue in these classes because the kids in "those" classes weren't like Jason. She further explained that Jason had a habit of running away and that she had a hard time controlling him at home.

At our request, she reluctantly agreed to sign a consent form so we could have Jason evaluated for special needs assistance. She was concerned with how long the process might take. We explained that we would try to hurry the process along, but that it might take at least a month to schedule all the assessments. In the interim, we agreed to stay in close contact with her. Mrs. Jamison agreed to call Sherry every day for the next two weeks to let her know how Jason was doing. To the relief of all of us, Jason got through day number two, Wednesday, without incident.

On Thursday, though, Jason's third day, he was referred to the office twice in the morning for swearing in class as well as talking many times without permission. After lunch he was referred to the office a third time for pinching the girl in front of him in English class, leaving a red welt on her arm.

I called Jason to my office and told him that his mother was being contacted to come pick him up since he had been referred to the office three times in one day. He would have to go home for the day and return with his mom the next day for a meeting. He didn't say anything as I dialed his home phone number. Just as I was finishing the conversation with his mother, Jason yelled loudly enough for his mom to hear, "I'm running away and there's nothing you can do to stop me," and he stomped off out my office door. Sherry was almost in a panic, pleading with me to go after him since he was so new to the area and she wouldn't have any idea of where to even begin looking for him. She said she was on her way to school and hurriedly hung up.

I sighed and went out into the hall. It was a pleasant fall day as I saw Jason go banging out the front door of the school and head off towards the cornfield that was about 300 yards away from the building. He was not running but was walking with his head down. About 100 yards to his left students from a science class were walking through the prairie grass area with large insect nets.

At the door, I hollered for Jason to stop, but he kept right on walking—pretty much what I expected. Not wanting him to reach the tall cornfield, I shook my head and ran to catch up to him. By now we were only about twenty yards from the school driveway, so I knew his mother would see us if she drove up soon.

I reached Jason, put my hand on his shoulder, and asked him to please wait with me for his mom since she was on her way to school.

"Take your hand off of me or I'll kick you," he said.

Well, being two years into my career as an administrator, I was certain he wouldn't actually kick a principal, so I said, "I am not going to let you go and I know you won't kick me."

I felt a hard blow to my shin—twice.

"How did you like that? If you don't let me go I will hit you!" And sure enough, he proceeded to pound me while I stood there holding onto him. Then he announced that he would spit on me. And he did that, too!

Still I clung to his shirt praying for his mother to arrive. He was wildly squirming now in an attempt to get away from me. Trying to get some help, I waved to the science teacher—who waved back and smiled! She thought I was just saying hello!

Finally Sherry's car came around the corner. At the same time a math teacher, whose classroom window faced where Jason and I were standing, came outside to help. The math teacher and I took Jason to the car and I explained to his mother what had happened. She was most appreciative of what I had done and said she would call me in the morning.

After they left, I called the central office to let them know what had happened. This hadn't been exactly a normal day. The assistant superintendent immediately came to my office and took notes as I related the incident. He was not too pleased that I had tried to physically detain Jason. He knew I was trying to help, he said, but I could have unintentionally hurt him, potentially getting myself in a lot of trouble.

I hadn't really thought about that while trying to keep my shins intact. The assistant superintendent asked me to write an incident report, putting everything in my own words, just in case the parents filed a complaint.

That night as I did what he had asked me to do, I thought deeply about what I could have done differently. Clearly, the assistant superintendent was right in that I could have unintentionally hurt Jason and could have then been in trouble. Jason could have made up a story about how I had hurt him even if I really hadn't. I then started to worry about what might happen the next day. I didn't sleep all night.

The next morning, the veteran teachers in the workroom told me that I was nuts to have gone after Jason and echoed many of the assistant superintendent's comments.

I waited for Sherry to call that morning. No call came. Jason didn't show up for school. After a while I called their house. The phone had been disconnected.

Incredibly, sadly, that's where it all ended. We never heard anything from them ever again. We were never contacted by another school for Jason's records, and with his having so little participation in our school, we sent them back to his previous school.

There is no way to avoid such unpleasant incidents when dealing with the amazingly broad spectrum of life in any community. The best that we can hope for, as educators, and as part of the human race, is to take from each encounter some lesson worth learning. I never again physically restrained another student, thereby risking doing them harm, unless they were attempting to harm another student.

I can only hope that Jason grew to find a path for himself that would lead away from the cornfield.

☎ Upset parent call about the decision to have school:

"Obviously no one in that office cares about the safety of our kids. We have school today and there is no way it is safe due to the snow. I am keeping my kids home because I think it is not safe." The secretary told the parent that it was perfectly fine for him to keep his kids home and that there would be no academic penalties for his decision. He then said, "Oh, so it is okay?" The secretary responded that of course it was okay since parents know what is best for their children's safety. He then wanted to know, "Will they be counted as absent?"

SHOW
AND TELL

*A high school speech class stretches
things to slip one over on the teacher.*

One day our outstanding speech instructor, Dan Rydel, received an unusual request from a student named Kevin. He wanted to do his final demonstration speech on the topic of the use of condoms. Kevin's justification for the topic was the AIDS crisis.

Dan Rydel was one of the best drama coaches and speech instructors in the metro area. His students competed in district, state, and national contests and were usually quite successful. We often received requests from other schools to visit Dan's class or get copies of Dan's curriculum as it was deemed very progressive and powerful.

By the time students reached Advanced Speech, part of the process was for students to peer-edit and critique speeches. The final speeches for the second semester of the class were made before the class and required the use of demonstrations and were videotaped to become part of each student's portfolio.

Dan was a very private person, and while speech and drama instructors tend to be extroverts, Dan was an introvert. He was very concrete and very sequential—about which he was the brunt of teasing from his students—but he put up with very little nonsense from them in class or at the podium.

The year that Kevin submitted his unusual speech proposal to Dan, the group of students in the Advanced Speech class was very good, but also very exasperating for Dan. He would comment to me from time to time that while these students had more talent than many in the past, he couldn't count on them to do what was expected and not goof around in his absence. They had, though, been doing an exceptionally fine job on their demonstration speeches.

Now here Dan sat fidgeting in my office with the proposal from Kevin. This was the first time as Dan's high school principal that I had seen him so flustered. He was asking me if I would allow him to approve Kevin's request to give a demonstration speech on the use of condoms as prevention for the spread of the AIDS virus. Kevin had assured Dan that he would not use any props other than a condom and that the purpose of his speech would be to explain how condoms were used to prevent sexually transmitted disease. His speech would focus on AIDS, how the disease was transmitted, and how it could kill a person. Kevin had already asked each member of the class to sign a release giving him permission to do the speech. The one student in class who was under eighteen had secured a written permission slip from her parents.

All the barriers were removed—so to speak. It was up to the administrators to decide.

Dan held a spirited debate with himself in my office. On the one hand, he was very reluctant to allow Kevin to do the speech that migh not be entirely appropriate for a high school audience. On the other hand, he was well aware of the seriousness of the issue and the importance of imparting this information, and he trusted Kevin. At length, he opened his debate for discussion and I got to participate. It didn't take me long to decide to give Dan permission to move ahead for two reasons: first, since all speeches were videotaped, we were confident that Kevin would keep his word that no other props would be used; and, second, there were no student objections. It was up to Dan, who decided to give the green light.

Kevin was scheduled to give his speech that Friday and I asked Dan if he wanted me to attend. He said he appreciated it, but that he didn't want to draw any more attention to Kevin's speech than any other. He promised to brief me Friday after school, which he did, in my office, as follows:

Kevin came to the front of the room carrying a small paper bag, which he set next to him and commenced his speech. He had charts that he referred to during his talk showing how AIDS attacked a person's immune system when the virus entered the body. He had put together an impressive PowerPoint presentation outlining current statistics on the

AIDS virus. The talk was very well researched, very well presented, and Dan was breathing a sigh of relief as it drew toward conclusion. In closing, Kevin stressed that even though a condom could help protect the spread of the AIDS virus, it was not a sure thing, the risk increasing if it were not put on correctly.

At that, Kevin reached into the paper bag and withdrew a condom. He opened the condom, displayed it, and began to explain in detail how it was to be used. It was a bit much, maybe, but overall Dan felt it would pass muster—right up to the point when, with no warning, Kevin reached back into the bag and produced a banana, which he proceeded to sheath with the condom in graphic demonstration of application.

Dan had kept his composure somehow, believing it might be more of a problem to stop the demonstration than to leave it alone. Kevin's speech concluded, he returned his props to the bag, and all the students clapped, saying that his speech was the best ever! Dan thanked Kevin curtly for the presentation, clearly put out.

Sitting now in the chair across from my desk relating the incident, Dan was fidgeting again; there was more to the story. I leaned back in my chair and laced my fingers across my middle resignedly. "Let's hear it," I said.

First, the student who had run the video camera told him after the speech that there had been a problem with the tape, so none of the speech was recorded. That was perhaps a mixed blessing, but what happened next was neither mixed nor a blessing: one of the other students lingered after class and told Dan that this had been their class's senior prank on him. The students had collected money and paid Kevin $50 to do his speech, knowing full well how Mr. Rydel would react.

At this point, Dan's concern was with the school board's reaction and reporters for the local paper hearing of the prank. He was a very proud teacher and was embarrassed that his students would play such a trick.

It was late Friday afternoon. There wasn't much to be done until Monday besides inform the central office in case any calls came in over the weekend. On Monday we would address his students, together.

When Dan was gone, I finally allowed myself a private chuckle. A banana!

Over the weekend, Dan reflected on the speech, ultimately concluding that none of the information had been presented in a vulgar manner. In fact, overall, it really had been one of the best final presentations given by any of his students. Too bad for Kevin that he had no portfolio piece to show for his work.

At a morning meeting, Dan explained his position to the rest of the English department. He felt that making a big deal of the matter could only escalate the situation and served no useful purpose. The other faculty agreed, as did I. We just let him deal with the class as he saw fit. The central office had not received any complaints nor had I.

And there were no further repercussions. Dan gave Kevin high marks.

Finally, on graduation day in June, Dan's Advanced Speech class presented him with a gift in thanks for being one of the best teachers they had ever had. It contained a gift certificate to a local restaurant, a common gesture of appreciation from students. But in the bottom of the box, under the gift certificate, was something else: a copy of the videotape of Kevin's speech.

Note from a middle school parent:

Your guess is as good as ours as to why Dave missed school yesterday. We left for work and he was ready for school. Then when we got home he was watching TV and said he had called school to tell them he was sick. He didn't look sick, but we weren't there in the morning to make sure. Go figure—it's your call if this is excused or not. Let us know.

ODYSSEY OF THE
MISCHIEVOUS MIND

Sometimes you just have to wonder,
"Who's really in charge here?"

"Odyssey of the Mind" was an annual school competition for bright students from the elementary grades through high school. We were fortunate to have two high school teams go through the local, state, and regional competition and win the right to compete nationally against other high school teams. Each year the finals were held at a university campus in late May, with the dorms used for housing contestants and chaperones.

The University of Colorado at Boulder, about a twelve-hour bus ride away, was the site for the upcoming finals. Some of our participating students had the reputation of being not only brilliant but also quite a handful. A group of the parents asked me, the principal, to chaperone the teams, saying it would make them feel more at ease. I agreed to take on the job.

The students and their parents signed a strict pledge to observe the rules on the trip, including observing school rules and not drinking, smoking, or fighting. If a student were to violate any of the rules, he or she could be sent back home on a plane at the family's expense.

Our teams were entered in robotics and a dramatic production. The competition was being held on a Thursday, Friday, and Saturday, with students returning on Sunday. So we packed our team bus with forty-two people and headed off to Colorado on Wednesday.

A day of competition ended with an evening of social activities. In fact, it was a very social occasion. Meeting others from around the country was a special treat for everyone, including the parents who had made the trip. Even sentry duty was enjoyable, as parents stood in the halls to prevent students from succumbing to temptation.

On Saturday, the seniors took part in a problem-solving competition. All the teams were given thirty minutes to solve the problem: on a wooden base, find a way to stack ping-pong balls and marshmallows as high as possible, using only toothpicks. The hitch was that each toothpick counted as a negative point. The teams drew for time slots, competing out of the sight of other teams so as not to share their secret strategies.

Our team, while inventive, brought the competition to a temporary halt because of how they stacked the ping-pong balls and marshmallows. Instead of using toothpicks, which were negative points, they tore apart the marshmallows and kneaded them, making them gooey, then used them like mortar as they stacked the balls. This worked beautifully, but left the ping pong balls covered with goo. The competition sponsors had to go out and buy new balls for the remaining teams. No one had thought about tearing the marshmallows apart, including the competition sponsors. Our team won the coveted Award for Creativity!

That was the only award we won, but it was the one every other team really wanted. After the awards ceremony was finished, we all went back to the dorms. The bus was leaving at 6:00 a.m. on Sunday morning and the students all claimed they were tired and just wanted to crash for the night. That should have been my first clue that they were up to something. I must have been lulled by the big award.

At about 1:30 a.m., the parent on hall duty decided to check on a few rooms—since things seemed just a bit too quiet—and discovered that *none* of the students were in the rooms!

As we should have known from their marshmallows gambit, these were no ordinary young adults; they were canny and mischievous and they knew perfectly well that we wouldn't send them home on a plane when we were leaving in the morning anyway. The other adult chaperones and I put our heads together and worked out different directions to take, then went off separately through the campus to look for our teams. I had taken a suggestion that I should canvas the area toward the quadrangle.

Since the night was quite warm, I was wearing just shorts and a t-shirt, and it would have been a very pleasant evening stroll under any other circumstances. As I passed another dorm building I suddenly spotted three of our students sitting on a park bench in a large park-like expanse of grass that was across the street. Relieved to see them, I called out to them, and they asked me to come over and join them—they were just talking about all the fun they had had on the trip.

I crossed the street and started across the fifty-odd yards of grass to join them. And the sprinkler system turned on. Like our precious and precocious students, these were no ordinary sprinklers! It was a powerful system designed to utterly drench the area in very short order. I looked up balefully, suspicious then, and through the sputtering spray was able to see that *all* of our students were now gathered at the park bench. The rest had come out of their hiding places and were laughing themselves silly because they finally had "got" their high school principal.

I marched through the gauntlet of hosing sprinklers and emerged trying in vain to shake myself dry. They confessed, between bouts of hilarity, that the day before they had located the sprinkler system controls in the basement of the dorm, changed the dial from automatic to manual, then tested the different switches and knobs until they found the one that controlled the area they wanted. They had all sneaked out of the dorm through windows and stairway exits, knowing I would have no choice but to come looking for them. I wasn't able even to put on a stern act and was laughing right along with them.

We walked back to the dorm, I got dried and changed, and everyone finally went to bed. It was a fun way to end the trip with no harm done. Most of the parents had been let in on the prank by the kids, which is how I had been given my searching assignment. I had sort of wondered why the other chaperones hadn't seemed more concerned when we noticed the kids missing from their rooms, but those little nagging things often tend to make sense only in hindsight.

It's awfully hard to get or stay mad at smart and good kids only trying to have a little good-natured fun. And besides: nobody wants to be a wet blanket.

MAN WITH A GUN

Lights and sirens to the track field!

Our small town did not have city garbage collection in the early 1970s. A retired railroad worker, Harold, owned a dump truck and contracted with local residents who wanted weekly garbage pick-up service. Harold was a quiet, odd man, almost a recluse. His clothes were generally clean but tattered. Rumor had it that he never used a bank and that he kept all of his money hidden somewhere in his house in an old tin can. Of course, no one knew if this was true or not, but it was a great story. Even the high school kids had heard the story.

The school system also used Harold's garbage service and he was allowed to park his dump truck at the school. Every morning Harold would arrive, park his old 1960 Buick next to the dump truck, and take the truck out for his town routes. Afterwards, Harold would pull his dump truck next to the high school between the track field and the building. The track field and the building were only separated by a downward sloping grass hill about twenty yards long, with a gravel driveway at the top of the hill that hugged up close to the building wall. Harold would back his dump truck down this gravel drive and park it near a set of doors where the custodians could empty the school garbage into the truck. This was his daily routine during the week.

High school students often would say "hi" to Harold as they came out for track practice, but Harold never responded to them or even looked in their direction. Over the years he earned a deserved reputation as being pretty ornery.

One afternoon our track coach approached as Harold was maneuvering to park his truck for the day and asked if he had any interest in helping at any of the track meets. Harold responded gruffly, "I never had any kids, don't like kids, don't think our tax dollars should help kids run around in circles, and I sure won't help at any track meets."

Utterly taken aback by Harold's harsh reaction, the coach responded, "Well, Harold, have a nice day. Sorry to have upset you." Harold put his truck in reverse, backed up next to his Buick, got out of the truck, hopped into his car, and left without saying another word.

The track coach stood and watched Harold go, scowling a bit. Coach was the type of person who felt, and made others feel, that becoming involved in the school was great for the kids and fun for adults. He had a lot of school spirit—which had just been trampled on by hobnail boots. Unfortunately for Harold, Coach also happened to be one of the best and most inveterate, incurable pranksters on the entire high school faculty, as many victimized faculty members could attest. And as he watched Harold speed away, the wheels began to turn. . .

The next week on Friday there was a track practice. We'd participated in invitational relays the day before. I was doing my usual rounds as administrator, chatting with one of the coaches, when Harold's truck came into view around the building corner at the top of the grassy hill, and he began backing down the gravel driveway.

Suddenly there was a commotion on that side of the field, at the bottom of the hill, and we saw Coach arguing heatedly with his shot putter, Tim—a big athlete, about 6'2", who also was the center on the football team. It wasn't immediately clear what the row was about. Their voices grew louder, and Tim suddenly wheeled and started trotting up the grassy hill toward the building as Coach yelled at him to get back down on the field at once. It was getting ugly.

Tim was completely ignoring Coach, trotting straight toward the building doors where Harold was just backing the truck into place. Furious now, nearly apoplectic at being ignored by his student, Coach yelled at the top his lungs, "I've had it with your smart mouth and insubordination!" And with that Coach pulled out a .45 caliber pistol and fired three times! Blam! Blam! Blam! The explosive shots echoed again and again against the building walls, and Tim, who was almost directly in front of the wild-eyed Harold's truck by now, clutched at his side and fell, writhing in agony, rolling over and over back down the grassy slope.

Everyone was frozen. Everyone but Harold, that is. All three of those shots had been coming almost directly in his direction! He slammed his truck in forward gear and sprayed gravel all over creation as he floored it to get out of there. He had disappeared around the corner of the building even as the coaches and I began to come to our senses and run toward the hill—and that's when Tim got up and started laughing so hard he could hardly walk. Coach was doubled over shaking with laughter. Soon everyone was laughing just as hard as they realized they had witnessed one of the funniest, if most brutal, practical jokes in school history.

It was just Coach's starting pistol full of blanks he had been firing. And Tim had given an Oscar-winning performance as the young victim.

Meanwhile, though, Harold was completely convinced that he had witnessed a real shooting and was extremely distressed. He had driven home at top speed and raced into his house to call the police and the superintendent of schools to tell them that the track coach had shot a student and that someone better get over there at once.

The town only had three policemen and it was the chief who arrived at the track in short order, lights flashing and sirens blaring. The superintendent came screeching into the parking lot about two minutes behind the officer. But when they arrived, they only found Coach and the team sitting on the ground laughing themselves to tears and reliving the story over and over again. Tim had become a major team hero.

They soon sobered up, however: the police chief didn't see it as one bit funny and neither did the superintendent.

Coach was led into the school to tell the whole story to the police and fill out a report. Then he had to call Tim's mother and tell her what had happened, admitting that he had used poor judgment in asking Tim to be part of the prank.

Next Tim and Coach were instructed to go to Harold's house to apologize. Harold refused to open the door, so instead they wrote him a letter of formal apology. Even then, Harold—in protest over Coach not being fired and Tim not being expelled—absolutely refused to pick up garbage from the school for a week. He finally relented, though, and came back to his old routine.

This story never made the media, thanks to the work of the police and the superintendent to keep it contained, but it gained almost mythological status at the school. It was told only once annually: on the anniversary of the event, at track practice the day after the big invitational relays, every year without fail right up until the year Coach retired. No one ever missed those practice sessions.

Note from a high school parent:

Sally missed school yesterday since it was Yom Kippur, a Jewish holiday. While we are not Jewish, Jewish kids get to stay home on our holidays, so we felt it appropriate for Sally to stay home on one of their holidays. Thank you.

FALSE ALARM

Smoking Wars Part III

Beth was elected student council president by one of the largest margins of any other student who had held this position. Beth was a great student council president but a bit of a wild card in regards to following school rules. She followed the letter of the law but walked right on the edge most of the time. This was probably why she garnered so many votes in the election; she knew all the groups of kids and everyone liked her.

Sue—the teachers' nemesis from Smoking Wars Part I—had brought her smoking habit with her to high school. Contrary to Beth, Sue was not well liked by the other girls in her class or at school. This was not good for her as a smoker because she didn't have a lookout to help her beat the system.

One day as I was standing in the hallway by the lunchroom, Beth approached me with a strange question. "If there were smoke in a room and you could not determine the cause at first and then you did determine the cause, would it be appropriate to grab an extinguisher, hit the fire alarm just in case, and extinguish the fire?" I told her that if there was a fire or she noticed smoke she should hit the alarm and tell the nearest faculty member or school employee and then exit the building. The school employee would then know what to do. She looked thoughtful and nodded.

I had to ask her why she was wondering. She told me that she was writing a report and wanted to include some information about protocol in the case of a student discovering a fire in school. I didn't give it much more thought until a week later when during my lunch supervision time the fire alarm went off and I could hear two girls screaming in the girls' restroom.

I rushed into the restroom to find Beth and Sue pulling each other's hair, ripping each other's blouses, slipping on the water that was all over the floor, and swearing like sailors, calling each other every name imaginable. Breaking up a girl's fight is always worse than a boy's altercation because girls don't quit when you try to get between them. There was a good deal of commotion going on with the fire alarm screaming, the girls fighting, and the rest of the students and faculty exiting the building. I finally managed to separate the two, at the cost of some flesh, and I took them outside until the alarm was silenced. I then marched the brooding pair to my office.

Sue was fit to be tied as she told her version of the story. "I was *using* the restroom, *sitting* on the toilet, *minding* my own *business* when the fire alarm went off and then someone dumped a *ton* of *water* over the top of the stall and absolutely *drenched* me! I pulled up my jeans—which were, like, *so wet*—opened the door and there's Beth! *Laughing* at me! Holding an empty garbage can! So I started to beat the crap out of her! Then you came in and that's all I know. Hey, you know, just because that bitch is the stuck-up student council president doesn't mean she can get away with this!" I told Sue to stay in my office while I went to listen to Beth's account.

Beth's story, of course, was different. She explained calmly, "I went into the restroom after I ate lunch and I smelled smoke. I asked if there was anyone in the restroom. No one responded. I quickly looked under the stall doors and saw no feet. I saw smoke coming from the stall next to the wall. Then I remembered our conversation about pulling the fire alarm so I ran out of the restroom and pulled the alarm, then went back in and noticed that the garbage can had some water in it. So I dumped it over the stall door to put out the fire. Then *Sue* came out swearing and *screaming* at me and calling me names and started throwing punches. I had to do something! So I grabbed her hair and blouse and we started fighting. You came in and that was that. I was just trying to put out what I thought was a fire in the stall." Then she cocked her head at me and smiled.

I managed something in return that probably qualified as a grimace. It was obvious to me that Beth had known very well that Sue was in the stall smoking and just wanted to get her good—so she did. Pulling a false fire alarm is a serious offense. But Beth never changed her story one bit and contended that she really thought there was a fire; being the student body president she felt she had a duty to protect others. Sue, on the other hand, remained completely furious about the entire situation and wanted Beth suspended or expelled.

I thought the whole thing through, then called both sets of parents and explained what each girl had told me. I also explained that I doubted we would ever get them both to come to an agreement as to the facts of the situation. The one fact that both could agree on was that they were fighting in school. As a result of that, each was suspended for three days for fighting. Sue was furious; Beth just smiled.

The girls never got into trouble again, but Sue continued to smoke in the restroom as she had done since middle school. We just never could quite catch her. Students talked about this story for years to come, even after both girls graduated from high school.

I never did ask Beth how the garbage can might have come to have water in it prior to the fire alarm sounding. Some questions are best left unasked.

Note from a middle school parent:

Our son John is in eighth grade and his girlfriend broke up with him this weekend. He was really upset so we allowed him to stay home yesterday. She is in three of his classes and we would like you to reschedule her classes so John doesn't have to see her. Please wait until the end of the week to start her new schedule in case they get back together.

A FAMILIAR PORTRAIT?

Know-it-alls never learn because
they already know it all.

There seems to be at least one know-it-all in every bunch. You know the type: the person who claims to know more about the subject at hand than anyone else present—even when they know nothing whatsoever about the subject. The know-it-all seems willing to go to any lengths to impress people, usually with the result of alienating them. Mr. Sullivan was a shining example.

He was a high school social studies teacher, and though he certainly did a serviceable job teaching his subject, in social situations and with faculty he could be the most infuriating boor. When it came to students' feelings about Mr. Sullivan as a teacher, there was no gray area; kids either really liked him or despised him. Most faculty, though, found it difficult to deal with him.

Some of his gaffs became almost legendary. One arose out of his additional duties as the junior high school girls' basketball coach. At a state-sponsored sports regulations meeting one evening, Mr. Sullivan introduced himself to the gathering as the high school varsity boys' coach, unaware that the high school varsity coach was also attending (but was seated in the far back of the room). The real varsity boys' coach didn't say a word, remaining quiet in the back of the room until it was his turn to speak. He stood, gave his name and school, then said, "I guess I will have to go back to my school to see why I was not told I am no longer the varsity boys' coach." The entire room broke out into laughter—with the exception of Mr. Sullivan.

But some people never learn.

During lunch Mr. Sullivan would listen to what other people were talking about and then chime in with his alleged experiences on the same topic. One semester I happened to eat lunch frequently at the same time as Mr. Sullivan. Some of his fellow teachers privately told me that no matter what article or book they discussed, Mr. Sullivan would claim to have read it, too, and would then give his synopsis of its true meaning. To demonstrate this to me, they decided to make up a fictitious book title about English teaching skills and discuss it during lunch period.

The next day, the teachers started discussing the fictitious book. Several minutes into the conversation, Mr. Sullivan spoke up to say that he had also enjoyed the book, especially the section about teaching the parts of speech to special needs students. The head of the English department looked over, interested, and asked him more about this section. Mr. Sullivan went into detail about what he thought the true meaning of that section really was. After a while, the teachers decided to give it up and told him that they had made up the book title just to see if he would do exactly what he had done. Mr. Sullivan stayed adamant about having read a book with that title, declaring that the book he had read must have been written by another author.

But some people never learn.

One day Mr. Sullivan quietly finished eating his lunch, but before leaving the lounge, he walked over to the art teacher who was seated on a couch wearing culottes. He boldly lifted up the front flap on her culottes and then let it drop back onto her lap with a smile. The art teacher stood up and from behind her lower back launched a roundhouse swing and slapped Mr. Sullivan squarely across the face. Staggering, he exclaimed, "I was only checking to see if they were culottes!" to which the art teacher replied, "That was just in case they weren't."

About ten minutes later Mr. Sullivan came to my office and asked if he could go home since he had a red handprint across his face and didn't want to have to explain it to his afternoon classes.

I waved him off to go home because some people never learn.

No matter how many times I tried to help Mr. Sullivan realize that he didn't have to try to be someone else or to stretch the truth about everything or show off to be accepted as "one of the group," he continued with many of the same antics until he retired.

✎ Note from a high school parent:

This will be complicated, but please listen carefully. I know you are just an attendance secretary so you may have to ask the principal if this is excused. Our daughter Linda attended a prom at another school this weekend. She finally got home Sunday afternoon at 4:00 p.m. and was really tired from not sleeping and drinking so much Pepsi-Cola. We allowed her to stay home Monday to rest. We know it was just so much Pepsi-Cola that caused her to be so tired no matter what else you hear. Is this excused?

SQUANDERED GIFTS

Native brilliance can cut both ways.

It all started when strident alarms sounded throughout the school as dense smoke began pouring into the hall from one of the boys' restrooms, and everyone in the school scrambled to exit the building. The alarms meant firefighters would already be rushing toward the school, so I checked to make sure the evacuation was moving smoothly, then went down the long hallway to check that the classrooms were empty.

I soon realized, though, that the smoke was dangerously thick, and I was forced to find a window to climb out through. I was greeted by a rather stern-looking firefighter who was not pleased with my decision to enter the smoke-filled hallway. I opened my mouth to assert that the students were my responsibility but immediately realized putting myself in jeopardy had been foolish. I thanked him and went on to my fire drill duties.

After the smoke cleared the firefighters went into school to search the area. An empty coffee can was found next to one of the toilets. It had been filled with some type of chemical mixture that itself created very dense smoke when ignited. The intensity of the fire in the can ignited the hard black rubber toilet seat, making the smoke even denser, similar to what's produced by a burning car tire. The remaining smoke in the building was exhausted with huge fans and the building was deemed safe for occupancy about an hour later. School resumed. The fire marshal provided me with as much information as was available following the investigation. The search then began for the perpetrators.

Clearly, the student or students involved in this had knowledge of chemistry. The fire department had provided a list of chemicals used to make smoke bombs, all of which would be found in the high school chemistry labs. The next step was to interview students who were scheduled to be in chemistry classes at the time of the incident who had been issued hall passes. One of these students, Patrick Williamson, was part of what we called the "team"—a close-knit group of boys, two from the Talented and Gifted (TAG) class, two from the neighboring class for "at risk" students. It was an unlikely group of friends, but their various talents, gifts, needs, and personalities seemed to complement each other, so they had become something of a force within the school, often pushing the envelope on school rules and regulations. When questioned, though, Patrick was able to demonstrate conclusively that he had been in the band room at the other end of the school at the time of the alarm. It seemed to prove that he could not have been the culprit.

All likely students were questioned, but the investigation stalled when all the suspects, just as with Patrick, could be placed elsewhere when the chemical smoke bomb had been lit. The assistant principal and I still felt convinced that the "team" had orchestrated the smoke bomb incident, but proving it was turning out to be difficult. Whoever it was seemed to have gotten away with it.

The following Monday at 5:30 a.m., the head custodian, who regularly unlocked the building in the early morning hours and opened corridor doors, reported that there had apparently been a break-in on the second floor of the science wing. Whoever did it had super-glued all the built-in locker combination locks and had liquid-nailed the hallway doors shut on either end of the science wing.

I dressed in a hurry that morning and went in early. When I arrived, the custodian had the hallway door opened. The vandal or vandals fortunately didn't know the most effective way to apply Liquid Nails to a door and had used it like caulk squeezed into the crack between the closed door and the jamb. Applied that way, the Liquid Nails could be easily removed and had not bonded the doors closed.

The lockers, nearly 100 in this hallway, were another problem. The combinations were frozen solid with the super glue and could not be moved at all. The only solution was for the custodian to drill out the center of the locks, allowing the lockers to open, but obviously not to lock. New locks were ordered.

The police were called and they took fingerprints from the window that had been used to enter the science wing of the building. Someone, it seems, had left the window ajar from the inside. That pointed to student involvement. The police estimated that since the Liquid Nails was pretty hardened, the perpetrator or perpetrators had entered the building sometime about 10:00 p.m. on Sunday evening. Other than that, there were few clues.

The student body was pretty excited about these events, and the pranksters were achieving almost outlaw-hero status. We were getting very little cooperation from students. Even those who normally would pass along information that might lead to the culprits were very quiet. The "team" still seemed our best bet, but there was nothing solid to go on.

Since it was the spring of the year, with graduation looming for seniors, many parents actually took the position that "senior pranks" were just a rite of passage, so we weren't getting much cooperation from them either.

The fire department didn't share such a sanguine view when it came to the smoke bomb; they felt that there had been real potential for serious injury. As a result, a $500 reward was posted in the school for information leading to the arrest and conviction of the person or persons involved in the smoke bomb incident.

It wasn't long before a student named Ross came into the office with information about the smoke bomb and science wing incidents. I explained to him that we needed more than just a name. We needed some kind of factual information that would be worth pursuing. Ross felt he had just that. The name he gave me was Patrick Williamson, the very member of the "team" who we had questioned early on about the smoke bomb, but who had a perfect alibi. I told Ross he needed to give me something substantial, really substantial.

As it turned out, Patrick was Ross's ex-girlfriend's brother. She had told Ross fairly recently that she was certain her brother had been part of the incidents since she had seen him sneak out of the house on the Sunday night before the science wing incident. She also saw him take a tube of super glue out from a drawer before he left. She even had directly heard her brother talking to his friends about how cool the smoke bomb was and that it was better than they had expected. Given that Ross had broken up with her, he no longer cared about keeping her secret, and since he could use the $500 for a car payment, here he was. I thanked him and told him I'd get back to him if everything checked out the way he had told it.

I briefed the assistant principal and James, the police liaison officer. Finally, we sent for Patrick Williamson.

Patrick was from the Talented and Gifted class. He had a perfect ACT score of thirty-six and had full-ride scholarship offers from four universities. He was an extraordinary young man in many ways but like so many gifted people had a maverick quality that had led him to the edge of trouble more than a few times. He was a bright kid and a smooth-talker but, like most teenagers, he was not real streetwise.

When he arrived at the office, James, who was very skilled at interviewing students, asked us to leave so he could speak to Patrick alone. It was only about half an hour later that James emerged and said that Patrick had taken full responsibility for both incidents. Patrick also insisted that he had acted alone. He said he had used a cigarette without a filter as a fuse on the smoke bomb, and that's what allowed him time to get to the band room before it went off.

Patrick's parents were contacted and asked to come to school. They were very upset with the boy and I didn't envy him when he left with them.

Later, the police gave Patrick a substantial fine and placed him on probation for a year. It was explained to him that if he had no problems with the law, during his one-year probation, his record would be cleared. Patrick then was given the choice of going through a school board expulsion hearing—which, if he were expelled, would go on his permanent record—or to go on our homebound education program. The homebound program would allow him to finish his classes, maintain his grade point average, and have an unblemished school transcript. While he would be unable to attend the graduation ceremonies, he would receive his diploma. He opted for the homebound program, a very smart decision for his future.

Patrick's untarnished record helped him in this situation. He never gave up any other names as having been involved, and there were no more pranks that spring.

Later, that summer, James pointed out to Patrick that he never asked for fingerprints to see if there was a match with those on the science room window. Patrick asked him why, and James told him that if they had matched, there was no way he could have done it alone: he couldn't have gotten to the window without help. Patrick smiled and just went on his way. He never did tell on his friends.

Note from an elementary parent:

Our son's name is Bentley and he is in the fifth grade in Mrs. Elmory's classroom. It was his turn to bring home the hamster for the weekend and, somehow, Monday morning, we couldn't find it since he left the cage door open Sunday night. I told Bentley to stay home and keep looking. He found it after lunch and called me at work. I told him I couldn't come and take him to school, so he missed the entire day. Tell Mrs. Elmory that she needs to get a new cage for the kids to use on the weekends.

THE FLOOD OF 1993

"Water, water everywhere, nor any drop to drink." —Samuel Taylor Coleridge

Des Moines, Iowa, has two rivers that join on the south side of the city. The Des Moines and the Raccoon Rivers provide unlikely city pleasures like boating, riverside restaurants, nature walks, trails, and fishing, but they also can present issues like flooding, pollution controls, safety, and general upkeep. The Des Moines waterworks, located in the city next to the Raccoon River, provides the majority of the water for the city and most of the suburbs.

I was superintendent of a nearby suburban school district, and we were among the communities that received its water supply from Des Moines. Water was pumped to our tower and then on to the residents and schools.

As with many modern-day conveniences, running water is something we simply don't think about being without. We are accustomed to simply turning on the faucet and having water there on demand. In June 1993, though, residents in Des Moines and the surrounding suburbs gained a new appreciation and respect for the convenience of running water.

It was June 11 and our high school was playing baseball in a neighboring suburb. As parents of a player, my wife and I were excited that our son's team was actually playing a game, since unusually frequent rains had cancelled many of the games during the early part of the season. This particular June day was beautiful, hot, and muggy, just right for an evening baseball game.

As we traveled on the interstate to the baseball diamond, we passed over the Raccoon River and noticed that the river was over its banks. Although this was not altogether uncommon at this particular bridge after periods of heavy rain, still, it seemed more swollen than I could remember. No media service had mentioned anything about serious flooding, though, so we didn't give it a lot of thought.

During the third inning of the game, all that changed. A police car drove up to the field in a position to command attention, and through a loudspeaker the teams and fans were informed by the policeman that the interstate used to get to the school's field had been closed, so we would need to take an alternate route home.

At the end of the game as we piled into the van with our two sons, we heard on the radio a warning being broadcast that the Raccoon River might come over its banks, spilling into the downtown Des Moines area.

There was another couple riding with us who worked downtown, and they asked if we would mind stopping by their workplace so they could pick up some things. By the time we got there, news reports were warning residents that both the Raccoon and Des Moines Rivers were dangerously high and that the point of junction of the two could flood in an instant. The junction of the two rivers was only about a quarter of a mile from where we had stopped for our friends. We sat waiting in the company parking lot with no more than two hundred yards separating us from the Raccoon River.

As we sat there, water started to run through the parking lot, and in a frighteningly short time it rose to about four inches deep. Our friends came running back, splashing through the flooding, while on the street pressure from the rushing water started causing man-hole covers to shoot upwards like Frisbees flying in the air. There was nearly a foot of water running in the street! The radio was warning that the roads leading out of the city's south side would be closed in a matter of minutes because of the river backing up into the storm drains.

All of us in the van were scared silly since we couldn't see where the now-open manholes were on the street, and we still had a quarter of a mile to go to reach the only bridge that could take us out of there. Then I noticed that there was a bubbling pattern to the water at intervals in the street. Deducing that that was where the holes were, we avoided those spots, got safely to the bridge, and were the last vehicle to cross that bridge for more than a week. As we continued on our way home, radio stations were providing emergency information regarding routes in and out of the city, peppered with continuous reports giving urgent updates and safety instructions.

When we finally arrived at home, there was a message on my answering machine from the city's mayor. When I returned his call, he told me that the waterworks in Des Moines, while protected from flooding by high berms and floodgates, could be compromised, and that while our area was high enough not to be flooded, we might lose our water supply. He suggested filling a bathtub with water as well as putting water into jugs in case that happened.

If we lost our water supply from Des Moines, the water tower would become the emergency supply for fires and the system would be shut off for all residents, including the school district. Fortunately, since it was summer, only summer school classes would be affected, should things come to that. At 2:00 a.m. things came to that: the mayor called back and said that the Des Moines waterworks had indeed been compromised and the water was shut down for all residents, including the schools.

We had heeded the mayor's advice and filled some jugs and the bathtub with water; we were thankful. The mayor expressed his hope that the waterworks would go back on line soon, but he had no prediction. And by morning, things were worse all over.

For my family in particular, our bathtub stopper evidently wasn't watertight because we woke to discover that there was no water in the tub. On the grander scale, the waterworks and much of Des Moines were under water in a serious emergency condition. The water level in some areas was at or above the tops of streetlights, and the turbulence of the rushing rivers was difficult for the human mind to grasp. Railroad ties were actually bent to look like pretzels as the water rushed over the railroad beds. Every aspect of this tantrum of nature was hard to fathom. This event had now become national news, and television networks were providing strategies to help residents deal with the situation.

As if things weren't bad enough, the rain started again. Residents of cities that were not flooded used this as an opportunity to collect as much rain water as they could to use for bathing and for pouring down toilets to flush them. In the flooded areas, of course, the rain only made things much worse.

The school district rented portable toilets for those employees who worked during the summer. As a good community partner, we allowed any employee who had an interest to go and volunteer to help in Des Moines with sandbagging. There were more than fifteen school district employees who pitched in every day. Since the schools had no water, summer school was cancelled until further notice, to the delight of most of the summer school students.

We were all beginning to grow accustomed to going to the city hall for allocated drinking water. Some stores took advantage of the situation by raising prices to astronomical levels for bottled drinking water, but the more decent and humane stores kept prices the same. For twelve days not a drop of water came out of a faucet for over 500,000 people. We learned to bathe in cold rainwater and make do with what we had, buying bottled water to drink, boiling water to cook with, and hand-washing dishes and laundry.

Finally, after those twelve unbelievably long days, the waterworks was restored to operation, water was turned back on, and people were able to resume their normal routines. The flooded areas were permanently marked, and today you can still see watermarks on light poles, trees with no foliage below the high water mark, and changes in landscaping to protect areas against future floods. The waterworks built higher dams around the facility, and other neighboring areas did the same.

In the fall when school started, many teachers used the opening day to ask their students what their families did during the twelve days without water. Regardless of the grade level, there were as many stories as there were students. What follows are some of the comments the students shared and recorded in their journals.

Second grade student: "I didn't like not flushing the potty after I used it each time. Before mom always got mad when I forgot—now I know why."

Seventh grade student: "It was cool—we got to drink pop all the time instead of water—my parents were freaking out since they didn't have water to make coffee. I told them to drink my Mountain Dew!"

Fifth grade student: "My dog didn't care since he drinks rain water all the time, but we had to keep the lids on the toilets down so he didn't drink you know what."

Eleventh grade student: "It was so not cool. I had to wash my hair in cold water. Try and get out the conditioner using cold water. It was terrible."

Kindergarten student: "We just went to my uncle's house in St. Louis and they had water there. When we got back the toilets would flush so we stayed at home."

Fourth grade student: "We boiled rain water so it was drinkable, but it tasted terrible, so we drove to the store and bought water in another town and it wasn't as bad. I liked drinking pop all the time and was kind of sad when the water came back on!"

Eighth grade student: "We had to brush our teeth using rain water and try not to swallow anything. I don't know how the people in the Wild West did that."

Third grade student: "My dad told my mom that he had to go out of town on business and was sorry to leave her with no water. She told him not to hurry home. I think she was really upset, but he came back."

Second grade student: "Did you know that you can only live without water for three days? My mom told my older brother that if he didn't just settle down that she wouldn't give him any of the water we bought. He said that he would die in three days if she did that. Mom told him that on day two she might change her mind."

Fifth grade student: "We really had fun. We stayed up late and read spooky books and drank pop since mom couldn't make lemonade or Kool-Aid. That was great."

First grade student: "We asked the fireman what he was going to use to put out a fire if there was one. He said the water tower had enough water to put out fires. How do they move that water tower to where the fire is?"

HOT AND COLD RUNNING TOILETS

Ouch!

Opening a new middle school was very exciting. After months of sharing space with the high school, our whole staff was eager to move into the new facility at mid-year. It was my first principalship, and being the first principal in a new building as well as having the opportunity to hire new staff was a great way to start this part of my career. What I should have kept in mind was to always expect the unexpected.

As we moved into the building, some kids complained about the water in the new drinking fountains not being cold enough. While I, too, thought that the water was a little warm for a water cooler, in the whole scheme of things it didn't seem like a big issue. Nonetheless, I added that concern to the long list of items to bring to the contractor's attention.

By mid morning of the first day, two sixth grade boys came into my office to report that the urinals in the boys' bathroom were "steaming." Since they didn't think it was "a good thing," they decided they ought to tell the principal.

A short while later, a female faculty member ask if she could see me, came into my office, shut the door, and said, "I know this will sound very odd, but when I was just in the restroom, there was considerable steam coming up from the toilet." I choked back my chuckle when I couldn't stop myself from visualizing the situation and managed to say soberly that I would call the contractor to report the problem.

A few minutes later the science teacher came into my office and asked, "Why are the hot water faucets cold and the cold water faucets hot in my science room?" I explained that the contractor was on his way and that there obviously was a problem in that area of the building, and just to have the students leave the sinks alone for now.

It turned out that a plumber had crossed the main two water lines going into that pod of the building: the hot was cold and the cold was hot.

By the next day it was fixed. The female teacher who had reported the steaming toilet came in later to thank me for not laughing at her as she had felt rather embarrassed having to tell me about it at all.

The students were excited that the drinking fountains now had water that was cold instead of lukewarm.

The science teacher was grateful that no one had been scalded.

The principal's imposing "to do" list got one measly line shorter.

Note from a high school parent:

Linda was absent for the past week due to the flu. She needs to make up all her work and we need to make sure she has ample time to do so as it usually takes her longer even when she isn't ill. I think she should have three weeks to make this work up. If you agree just tell Linda; if you don't, call her father. He lives in Chicago and we are separated.

DISHONESTY

A teacher just doesn't quite tell the truth!

When you are the new high school principal, people make appointments—many before the school year starts—just to get to know you. Most of the appointments made by faculty members are related to some specific purpose, but the underlying reason, really, is to check out the new person. Having had a few new starts as a principal, I easily recognized the ploy by now but didn't mind at all meeting with any of the faculty for whatever purpose.

As well as the "meet and greet" appointments, there were always teachers who wanted to see the new principal to discuss serious issues that they felt hadn't been properly dealt with by the past principal or the school administration.

In my first week at this suburban high school, Linda Clements came to see me to present me with a list of concerns. She was a member of the social science department and had been very frustrated by how she was being treated, not only by her department head, but by other faculty members in her department as well. She felt that there was no respect, no trust, no honesty, and no one listening to her concerns, even though she had been a teacher in the district for twelve years.

After listening to specific examples of each area of listed concern, I told Ms. Clements that I would speak to the department head, Ms. Thornton, to make sure she was aware of these concerns. Linda Clements seemed hesitant about me being the one to bring her concerns to Ms. Thornton, but she also said that she thought it was necessary. She hoped that the new school year could get off to a fresh start that way, and that things might have a chance to improve with a new building principal trying to help the department "click."

Ms. Thornton had won major awards for her social science teaching and was sought after as a presenter to other schools and faculties. When we met the first time, she took me off guard by asking if Linda Clements had been in to see me yet with her yearly concerns. When I looked puzzled, she handed me an old list from Ms. Clements almost identical to the one she had given me.

Ms. Thornton then volunteered that while it wasn't her job to evaluate Ms. Clements (it was mine, though she didn't say so), the former principal had not taken the time to investigate what was really happening in Linda Clements's classroom. He never checked out her excuses for not turning in reports on time, having late report cards, and excessive absences without proper excuses or prior notifications. I could clearly see that there was a communication gap between the department head and Ms. Clements, and, furthermore, there was no love lost between the two.

I said I'd better make an appointment for all three of us to talk so that we could avoid playing the "she said—no, she said" game. I tentatively scheduled the meeting with her for the following week. Ms. Thornton seemed thrilled to have the opportunity to iron out some of these issues. When I called Ms. Clements, she was not happy at all about the meeting and asked if she would be required to attend since her new contract had not officially started yet. I told her that on that basis she did not have to attend, but that I would move the meeting to after the teachers returned from their summer break, at which time it *would* be required. She said, "Thank you." I hung up the phone and just looked at it.

A few weeks later we had the meeting. Unfortunately, it went just about as I had expected. There were a lot of incidents that were exhumed from the past, and Ms. Clements and Ms. Thornton both made sure they got in their own little digs at each other. We finally agreed that it would be best to make sure that good communications took place going forward, and that they were not to let problems go on indefinitely and fester. I offered to sit with them if they needed help discussing issues, but encouraged them as adults to hammer out most of their differences themselves.

After that, things went relatively smoothly—at least for the first nine weeks. Then the parent-teacher conferences were upon us. Ms. Thornton made a point of telling me that Ms. Clements had always found a way to be absent for the evening sessions when most of the parents were available and the arena-style conferencing took place. In that format, parents came to the lunchroom, where each teacher was seated at a table, and that kept parents from having to go all around the building to talk to the teachers they wanted to see.

I later saw Ms. Clements and mentioned that I understood that she had missed the last two arena night conferences but hoped that she would be present this year. She smiled and said, "Of course." That night, as I walked around the lunchroom visiting with parents and introducing myself to as many as possible, I noticed a note tent on Ms. Clements's table saying that she had been in a car accident and would have to make special appointments with any parents who wished to see her.

In the natural order of things, Ms. Thornton happened to be sitting at the next table, so I was fortunate enough to get treated to, "I told you something would happen."

I was hoping that Ms. Clements's car accident was minor and that she was not seriously injured. The next day I stopped by her classroom before classes started and asked her what had happened. She explained that she was on her way to the conferences when she witnessed a terrible accident, so she stayed at the scene as a witness. She had called the office from a pay phone to tell the secretary to put the note on her table so parents who wanted to see her could sign up for conferences.

I asked her for the time and location of the accident and she gave me details. I said offhandedly that my cousin was the sergeant in charge of traffic accidents and that I was going to check on her story. She became furious with me for doubting her story and accused me of being unprofessional. She also asked to have a union representative meet with me before I made any phone calls. That pretty well confirmed for me that her accident report was no more real than my cousin, the sergeant.

That afternoon during Ms. Clements's planning period, she and her union representative came to my office to discuss the phone call I was going to make to the police department as a result of my questioning the legitimacy of her story. The union representative questioned Ms. Clements and she stuck with her story until the representative said to me, "As the principal you are going to look very foolish when you call and find out that Ms. Clements was in fact a witness at this accident scene. Let's just make the call and put it on the speaker phone." I said it was fine with me and lifted the receiver to dial, wondering how in the world I was going to fake the cousin part.

At this point Ms. Clements ask that we not make the call. She admitted to lying because she just didn't feel like attending conferences because there were always so many parents who seemed not to like what she was doing with their kids. The union representative climbed down off her high horse and asked me what would happen next. I said that I would be writing up the incident and it would be placed in her personnel folder. This would be her verbal warning and first write-up combined, and the next demonstration of insubordination could be grounds for more serious discipline up to and including a recommendation for termination depending upon the seriousness of the incident.

Ms. Clements said nothing further. For the next two years, she attended every conference and did exactly what the department head asked her to do. When Ms. Thornton asked what had happened to change Ms. Clements attitude so much, I just told her that we had come to an agreement that I really couldn't discuss. It was a personal matter.

I didn't ask her if she had heard about my cousin on the police force.

Note from an elementary parent:

Sally was not in school this morning because we went shopping. We missed the Sunday sales and wanted to see if anything was left.

ENDINGS PRECEDE BEGINNINGS

Continuing education in the classroom of life.

Life is the greatest educator, and one of its greatest lessons is for us to keep our hearts open to the possibility that every experience has a lesson and everyone we meet can give us insight.

Denise Larson, my assistant principal in a suburban high school, taught me invaluable and timeless lessons about strength, courage, and perseverance in the face of adversity during the two brief years we worked together.

In the fall of 1987 I had been a high school principal for seven years and had accepted a new high school principalship in a well-known and academically rich suburban high school. Denise had already completed one year as the assistant principal there when I began, and in that time had established herself as a strong educational leader. She was a good disciplinarian and was also well liked by the students, faculty, and community—a rare and tricky combination. She was clearly on her way to being a building principal. We established a rapport immediately.

As we divided responsibilities for teacher evaluation, discipline, and basic assignments, we realized that our strengths and weaknesses complemented each other. This made us a very strong team and one that the faculty soon recognized as special. The principal I had replaced had been in the position for fifteen years and therefore had hired most of the current faculty. Their loyalty to his administration was something that I knew would take some time to win over, and Denise was adept at helping the process along.

Denise was married and very happy with her life. She and her husband approached life in a manner that was healthy, exciting, and fresh. They were always fun to be around.

That fall our football team was ranked number one in the state for the large schools and everyone in the school and the community shared in the excitement. Our crowds for home and away games were huge. The press, college scouts, and loyal football fans loved watching our undefeated team. Denise and I, along with our spouses, traveled together to several of the away games and became even better acquainted outside of the school setting.

It certainly appeared that everything was off to a great start that school year, but on November 1, 1987, that changed dramatically. That day Denise and I were in my office revising second semester schedules when a phone call came in for Denise: the high school secretary interrupted us to tell us that someone from the local hospital was calling. There had been an accident.

Denise dropped her pen and rushed to the phone. She was told to come to the hospital immediately. Her husband had been in a serious accident.

We left at once. The trip to the hospital that normally took twenty minutes only took us ten. We drove silently, each with our own thoughts, Denise staring out the car window.

A good friend of mine was the doctor in charge of the emergency room in the hospital. I was relieved to see him when we arrived. As we rushed into the emergency area and Denise went to the desk to ask for help, Dr. Bright caught my eye from across the lobby and very slightly shook his head. A rush of cold crept into the pit of my stomach and I knew then that Denise's husband had died.

Dr. Bright led us into a private room where he sat Denise down and broke the news to her gently but firmly: her husband had died at the accident scene. I sat next to Denise. With shaking hands she reached into her purse and took out her address book and turned to a page. Her best friend was a teacher in another suburban district and I knew her well. We called her and asked her to come to the hospital.

Within a few minutes the coroner came into the room and handed Denise her husband's wedding ring and watch. Denise accepted it but she hardly seemed to be seeing anything. The coroner was a grandfatherly man and told Denise that she needed to see her husband. He was unmarked from the accident and the coroner said this was something she needed to do for herself. Preliminary indications were that her husband had suffered a massive heart attack while driving, and the nature of it was such that even if he hadn't been driving, even if a full team of heart surgeons had been with him at the time of such an attack, they would not have been able to save him.

Denise agreed to go with the coroner. It wasn't long before she returned, tightly gripping her husband's wedding ring, tears streaming down her face. The truth of what had happened had penetrated the veil of disbelief that tends to descend over us all in such traumatic situations. Drying her tears, she became focused on contacting their families, and she insisted on making the calls herself. As I heard her conversations, I absolutely marveled at her strength and her ability to relay the tragic news in ways that gave greatest comfort to whoever she was speaking with.

I made the calls to the school and central office staff. Denise's best friend arrived at the hospital and they hugged for a long time. They both were crying and holding each other while Denise told her friend everything she knew up to that time. Her friend then sat with Denise and they just held hands. After a few minutes, Denise opened up her address book and started making calls again.

About an hour later Denise and her friend left the hospital and I went back to school. The office staff, faculty, students, and community all mourned Denise's loss. She had touched so many hearts and now she was the one who was hurting.

About a week after the funeral Denise returned to school. She had lost weight and looked very tired. Family members had been staying with her. The students in the school had placed a banner on her office door welcoming her back. Students have a way of putting terrible things into perspective pretty quickly, and they are the best therapy a person can have in times like these.

Each day was a little better for Denise. One day after school, she told me that her husband, who had been diabetic, had complained of flu-like symptoms a few times for about four months prior to his death. The autopsy indicated that he had had some previous minor heart attacks that he thought had been the flu. She then said that the night before his death they had stayed up late talking about their future and about starting a family. I walked her out to her car and she said with tears in her eyes, "This will be my first night going home alone to an empty house." I asked her if she would like me to follow her home and stay with her for few minutes. Denise thanked me very kindly but said, "Then tomorrow will be my first time going home to an empty house—I have to get through this alone and postponing it won't help." I smiled in understanding, but it struck my heart hard as we said goodbye and she drove away.

Of course it took time, but really it wasn't long before each day found Denise infusing it with more of her special brand of magic and skill in making things run and in helping to shape the destinies of the young people who were our charges.

The next school year proved to be another one that would change Denise's life forever, but in a far different way than the first that I had spent working with her.

Denise's friends had been trying, with the best intentions, to include her in social events where there were single people as well as couples. She joked with me about their efforts and insisted that she really wasn't ready for dating.

Then one day, with Denise reluctant but barely willing, a close and insistent friend set up a blind date for Denise with a man from another city in town on business. She was very nervous about it but had spoken to the man several times on the phone and had liked him. She had asked him if he would be willing to come to our office and pick her up for a casual after-school "meeting," as she called it. He had cheerfully agreed. Everyone in the office was very anxious to meet him. Denise was cautious at best.

When he arrived he was holding flowers in hand and seemed every bit as nervous as Denise if not more. The rest was pure fairy-tale stuff.

Everyone has heard of and seen movies about love at first sight, but it's something else to see it "up close and personal." It was as though they had been looking for each other forever. To my great loss, Denise actually resigned her position as assistant principal and moved to the city where her new love worked, but who could blame her. She had no trouble securing an assistant principalship there. They were married, and now they have a wonderful daughter and are as happy as can be!

When her world had been darkest, Denise never allowed that darkness to take control. She never let her tragedy stop her from seeing the value of happiness, of good works, and of compassion for others. She taught me lessons I'll never forget.

Denise is one of the best middle school principals in the Midwest and now lives in a university city with her husband and daughter.

The memory of her smile still lights up the day.

Note from a high school parent:

Next week we will be going to Canada as a family on a holiday fishing trip. We are, of course, quite excited. Jason says that he will be missing three tests and that he is supposed to make these up before we go. I question this practice as then he would know what is on the tests and could tell his friends before they see the test. Did you ever think of that? We think it better that he takes the tests when he returns. Thank you.

OHHHHH, SISTER!

Nobody calls a nun at 5:30 in the morning—except me!

Some churches, businesses, and schools have established "calling trees"—lists of people for each participant to contact by phone—to ensure that people get important information quickly. Calling trees for schools are established particularly for emergency situations that arise in the early mornings and late evenings when school is not in session.

When a decision is made to cancel school or start it late because of weather, a district has a predetermined routine that usually includes two or three people who get the calling tree started. Canceling the public schools also meant that the parochial schools would close since our school district transported both public and private school children. As a new superintendent in Wisconsin, it fell to me to make the cancellation or late-start decisions for our district.

At the start of the school year, I received a call from Sister Ruth, administrator of the local Catholic school system. She was calling to ask if she could be added to the district's calling tree. In the past, she had had to listen to the radio or television on inclement mornings to learn of delays or cancellations. For reasons I couldn't understand, the previous superintendent had told her that he had too many calls to make to also include her name on the list.

I told her I would be glad to call her and asked her to give me a phone number where I could be certain to reach her in the very early morning. She was added to the district calling tree list for the calls that I made.

We only had three mornings that year where we had to start school two hours late. When the first one came up, after talking to the people I relied on for weather information and advice, I made the decision to start late because of icy road conditions in some areas. I started calling the names on my calling tree list. I decided to contact Sister Ruth first so she could get a start on her list.

It was 5:40 a.m. when I dialed, and it was only after several rings that a frail, female voice finally answered the phone. The conversation went like this:

"Good morning, may I please speak to Sister Ruth?"

"She is currently sleeping, as was I. Can she call you back a little later?"

I opted for a little further explanation: "This is the superintendent of schools and I need to speak with Sister Ruth regarding the weather and school."

The frail voice then said, "Well, what is the weather doing and why is it so important this early in the morning?" This question was not exactly impertinent, but it was not what you expect from a nun.

I took a long breath. Who knew it was so difficult to wake a nun? I decided that I needed to be more direct and said, "Sister, please wake up Sister Ruth so I can tell her that we are going to delay the starting of school today for two hours."

"Oh," she said. She turned away from the phone and yelled, "Sister Ruth—there is a **man** on the phone who wants us to start school late this morning. Do you want to talk to him?"

A few seconds later Sister Ruth came to the phone and apologized, "I'm so sorry about that. I should have told Sister Helen that you might be calling and that it was okay to wake me up. She is very protective of me."

I explained the weather situation to her and laughingly said, "Sister, if it takes this much to wake you up each time we delay school, no wonder you weren't on the calling list!"

She laughed and assured me that in the future she would take the early morning calls herself. And the good Sister was as good as her word.

✏ Note from a high school parent:

We want to express our concern for the amount of assignments that our son is receiving from chemistry class. Every night he has homework and it takes him most of the evening to complete it. At conferences the teacher said he doesn't turn in all of his assignments, but he spends each evening doing his chemistry so we don't know what the teacher is doing with his homework. Please check on this and call me.

COLD EYES OF
A KILLER

Who, today, will occupy the chairs
that face a principal's desk?

Discipline problems at the middle school level usually consist of minor offenses such as pushing, hitting, swearing, tardiness, smoking, and talking back. While there is some fighting, it usually isn't too serious and, most of the time, a bloody lip or a torn shirt is the worst consequence.

One May during the last week of school, a mother registered her two seventh grade boys. They were a couple of years apart in age, and one son had been held back in an earlier grade. The family had just moved to town and she wanted her sons, Matt and Troy, to make some friends prior to summer break. Obviously no grades would be given or any books issued as there were only a few days left in the school year.

The middle school students walked to the high school each day to eat lunch because the middle school lunchroom was not yet completed, passing into my view through a floor-to-ceiling window.

One Tuesday morning, I was on the phone when I saw the new student, Matt, exit school through the door next to my window. He took out a cigarette, lit it, and proceeded to smoke it right in front of me. I immediately hung up the phone, walked outside, and escorted him back to my office. I then called his mother to come and get him and asked that she keep him home for the rest of the week, since Matt obviously wasn't interested in following school rules. She argued, "Boys will be boys," but came to get him. I anticipated that Matt's eighth grade year would be an interesting challenge.

When school started the next August, Matt and his brother Troy both registered for school and got off to the same start as everyone else. The middle school lunchroom was scheduled to be completed later in the fall, so we were still walking to the high school for lunch. During the second week of school, while about 200 students and I were making our daily journey to the high school lunchroom, I heard quite a commotion and yelling at the front of the group.

As I hurriedly approached a crowd of students at the front of the group, I saw students circled around Matt and another student, and I heard kids yelling at Matt to stop. I pushed my way into the circle to find Matt on top of another eighth grade student hitting him repeatedly in the mouth as hard as he could. There was blood everywhere. I shouted for Matt to stop, grabbed him by the shoulders, and pulled him backwards in an effort to stop the seemingly one-sided fight. Matt turned and attempted to strike me until he saw who I was, and then he pushed me backwards and took off running.

The student on the ground was crying and both of his front teeth were broken. I told the students standing around to go to lunch, then I walked the boy to the nurse's office and called his mother while he was seen to and cleaned up. This student had never been in any trouble at school. He obviously was scared. He was quiet, shy, and a very bright young student. I asked him what had happened. He said all he knew was that out of nowhere this kid turned him around and started hitting him for no reason. The nurse finished cleaning him up and his mom arrived soon to take him directly to the dentist.

Per our school policies, I needed to hear Matt's side of the story right away. I called Matt's mother to inform her of the incident. I also called the police to let them know that a serious fight had occurred on school property and that the student was somewhere in the community. The police indicated that they had had a few dealings with Matt over the summer and, unfortunately, were very familiar with him.

That afternoon, Matt's mother brought him back to school. I interviewed him to get his side of the story. He said that his friends had told him that the kid he hit had been talking "trash" about him and he didn't have to take that, even if he had not heard it himself. When asked, he said he could not remember who the kids were that told him this. As I sat listening to this "justification" for a vicious and violent attack on a quiet, shy, pleasant boy, it struck me that Matt was one of the most coldhearted persons I had ever met. He showed no remorse whatsoever for harming the other boy and he seemed to look right through me when I talked to him. He was very different from any other student I had ever dealt with.

I told Matt and his mother that the beating was the worst I had ever witnessed in a school, and I described the boy's serious injuries.

Matt's mother had so far remained quiet during the conference. When I finished speaking, she asked if the school was going to pay for Matt's shirt since I had ripped it.

I don't know exactly what well of patience we, as educational administrators, are granted the grace to draw from at times like these, but I managed to indicate calmly that under the circumstances, there were more serious issues besides Matt's ripped shirt. I suspended Matt for three days and told the family that I would ask the superintendent to extend the suspension to ten days. I went on to explain that during the suspension, school officials would be analyzing the facts to determine if an expulsion would be recommended to the school board.

Matt's mother became furious. I was overreacting to the entire situation, she said. I tried one more time to get her to grasp the serious nature of Matt's assault on the boy and impressed upon her that the welfare of all the students in the middle school was part of my responsibility. Matt's actions threatened the safety of all students. As she stomped out of my office with Matt, she launched a Parthian shot over her shoulder, saying acidly that I had not heard the last from her.

The high school principal, the superintendent, and I reviewed the case. The team approach ensures that even if one party is emotionally engaged in the event, the student will still receive fair treatment. The team recommended a proposal to the school board that Matt be expelled for the remainder of the school year. His fight was deemed serious and a danger to the safety and welfare of the victim and, potentially, other students.

The school board held the hearing and Matt was expelled. His mother withdrew Troy as well and the family moved out of state. It was

September 1974, and I guess I had heard the last from Matt's mother, but as for Matt, I would be hearing from him again.

In the spring of 1988, while I was a high school principal in another suburban district, three detectives came to see me. I had a great working relationship with the police department, and it was unusual for them to come to my office without calling.

One of the detectives was from the state Department of Criminal Investigation (DCI). The other two were DCI detectives from a western state. They needed to see me about a very serious case they were working on in their home state. The story they told me was heartbreaking.

Matt, the former middle school student, had been in prison for robbery and then had been paroled. After his parole he robbed a store at gunpoint and on the way out of the store shot two people, killing one. The police surrounded the house Matt went to and finally arrested him. He was handcuffed behind his back and placed in the back seat of the patrol car. Two officers sat next to him on either side. Unfortunately, they had not frisked him well enough to discover another weapon concealed in his belt at the small of his back. By the time they got to their destination, Matt had worked the gun out of his belt and tried to shoot the officer to his left. The officer grabbed the gun just in time, and as Matt pulled the trigger, the hammer struck the fleshy part of the policeman's hand between his thumb and forefinger, which stopped the firing pin from striking the bullet that likely would have killed him.

The court later found Matt guilty of murder in the convenience store killing and the sentencing phase was coming soon. The detectives explained that to recommend the death sentence in their state, the person must be deemed incorrigible. This meant that the detectives had to build a history going back in Matt's life as far as records existed to make their case for the death sentence. Their question for me was whether I had any records regarding Matt's brief attendance during his eighth-grade year. They had the record of the expulsion notice, but the details were not on file.

I told the detectives that since 1973 I had kept notes in my planner detailing anything that was funny, sad, or unusual so that someday I might write a book about it all—the very notes that formed the stories you've been reading. I had notes I had taken during the incident leading up to Matt's expulsion and could give them an account of what I considered to be one of the worst beatings I had ever witnessed. They took me home to get the planner and we returned to my office. I made a copy of the entry and they listened to my recollection of the events and took their own notes.

They informed me that I might have to testify in person and, if so, would be contacted sometime during the next six months. We shook hands and they left.

As I sat down in my chair, I shuddered, recalling the cold, empty stare Matt had given me back in September of 1974. Clearly he was a very troubled person. The detectives never called me back, and to this day, I have no knowledge of Matt's sentencing results.

Cell phone call from a middle school parent:

"This is Mrs. Sullivan, and Carter will be absent today as he just threw up all over the dashboard as he was getting out of the car to go into the school. We are leaving the parking lot now—oh—he just threw up again! Bye!"

LITTLE
BROTHER

To give is to get back a thousand fold.

When my youngest son left for college and my wife and I experienced the "empty nest" syndrome, I started thinking about how to use my extra time to give back to education and the community. Around that time, I passed a billboard advertising the Big Brothers Big Sisters organization. Then soon afterward, a commercial came over the radio advertising how to become a Big Brother or Big Sister to a youth in need. The commercial said that the waiting list was long and that there were many children needing help. It intrigued me that I saw the billboard and heard the commercial at the very moment I was seeking a way to contribute.

I reviewed some information from the agency and discussed the program with my wife, who was very encouraging and felt it would be a worthy cause. I made an appointment at the agency.

The intake counselor was very friendly and reviewed the application with me. I provided references, went through a home visit, then waited to hear if I would be accepted into the program.

A week went by and the agency called to say that I was approved as a Big Brother and that I should come to the agency to meet with a caseworker and review files for potential Little Brothers. When I went to the meeting the caseworker had matched my likes, dislikes, hobbies, and activities with five children ranging in ages from seven to fourteen. She reviewed each child's folder without using names or telling me where they lived. We narrowed the list down to two children, one age ten and the other age fourteen.

I chose the fourteen-year-old, who, as it happened, was a freshman in high school in the district I superintended. The next step in the process was for me to meet with the boy's mother and allow her to interview me, because the mom also has to agree to the match.

Jonathan had been in the program for two years and had already had two other Big Brothers, neither of whom completed their commitment with him as Big Brothers. This, of course, had really hurt his feelings. His mother had raised him alone since he was nine months old and was very anxious that he have a male role model in his life. She was also concerned that he could not withstand abandonment by another male.

In my lifetime I have performed professionally in front of thousands of people, spoken to thousands of people, and been in many situations where it was normal to be nervous. You would think I had learned to handle nerves, but just thinking about this meeting gave me the jitters. When the afternoon came to meet Paula at the Big Brother offices, I was a bundle of nerves. We were introduced and sat together in the caseworker's office. As Paula began telling me about Jonathan and their life together, I was surprised by a number of coincidences. Her son's name had the same first letter as both my sons' names. His birth date was the same as my wife's. Like me, he was a musician, and he even played the saxophone just as my boys did. In addition to all that, Jonathan loved sports and was artistic and very intelligent, but he also was very insecure.

Paula and I talked for an hour and then I asked the caseworker what the next step was. The caseworker looked over to Paula and asked her if she would agree to this match. She looked at me, smiled, and said, "Jonathan cannot withstand another Big Brother who runs out on him. I ask that you promise to stay with him for two years. If you don't and you break his heart, I will never forgive you." I smiled and told her that I would agree to that commitment and would love to be Jonathan's Big Brother.

The next step was to meet Jonathan at his home and make an arrangement to do something together. He only lived about a mile from my home and I was very nervous about meeting him for the first time. But I put on my "teacher's hat" and headed over to his house.

There was really nothing to have been nervous about. Once the introductions were over, we were at ease with each other. Jonathan was on the freshman wrestling team at the time of our first meeting and had just arrived home from practice. Not surprisingly, he was hungry, so he and I drove through the fog into the city to a fast food place, then spent the evening eating hamburgers and talking.

I didn't have to be concerned about a lack of conversation; Jonathan was anxious to tell me about himself. We talked about everything, jumping from topic to topic. That simple evening was the start of a relationship that changed both our lives.

A requirement of the Big Brothers Big Sisters agency is to meet and spend time together at least twice a month. Jonathan and I agreed that Wednesday nights would be our nights together and that we would try to do some educational things as well as eating out, plus some fun activities, such as going to movies. Paula was strict when it came to movies. Jonathan could not attend any "R" rated movies unless the rating was for violence—not for language or sexual content. Since both Jonathan and I like action movies, I would first take my wife to a movie to check it out, then I would take Jonathan to the movie, assuring his mother that I had already seen it.

My family is in a socioeconomic bracket that is often referred to euphemistically as "comfortable." I was moving between two completely different worlds every week. Paula had a home that was modest but clean and well-kept. Besides her normal day job, she was an area supervisor for one of the newspapers that was delivered each Tuesday night. Jonathan had to get home from wrestling early on Tuesdays to do a route and help his mother. He was a very hard worker and I never heard him complain about helping his mom. They needed the income to support the family. The things I took for granted, Jonathan viewed much differently. He was always worried about making ends meet and never wanted to ask his mom for anything that might cause her to do without. He was teaching me more than I could have imagined about the struggles of families with moderate to low incomes.

The caseworker had mandatory meetings with me during the first year to make sure everything was going well. She also met with Paula routinely to ask the same questions. It was clear to everyone that Jonathan and I were a good match and becoming very good friends. We talked a few times each week and went out somewhere together almost every Wednesday. We also talked when I visited his high school—he didn't mind as long as I didn't embarrass him in front of friends, of course.

Jonathan was an honor student and a science whiz. He had scored a perfect 36 on the science section of the ACT when he was in eighth grade. His grades were top-notch except in English, which he hated. We always kept school a focus of our friendship in addition to discussing the normal stuff friends talk about. I also noticed Jonathan becoming more confident as an athlete and as a musician.

In the spring of Jonathan's junior year, my youngest son was graduating from college. At the same time, I was offered a job in another state. I had in fact fulfilled the "contract" I had committed to with Jonathan, but we had a very strong bond and the prospect of being separated from him was not easy. On one of our Wednesday nights in March, though, I sat him down and showed him a map of Wisconsin where I had circled a city. I explained to him that I was going to move that summer but would see him often because my wife's family was still in the area and we would be coming back to visit them. I was so afraid that he would break down.

But Jonathan said that he had been trying to find a way to tell me that he wouldn't be around in the summer, either, because he had decided to join the Army National Guard and do his basic training before his senior year. That way he would be in great shape for football and have that out of the way so when he graduated from high school, he could then go to college with a monthly commitment and two weeks in the summer. I knew that Jonathan had explored the Army National Guard as a means of helping himself develop into a young man and to help pay for college, but I hadn't known he had made the decision. I was relieved that we both had plans and Jonathan didn't seem as upset as I thought he might be. I know he was disappointed, but he believed me when I said I would never lose contact with him and would see him often.

That summer my wife and I moved and Jonathan went to boot camp. He did well, as we all had expected he would, and came home in great shape for football. We talked a lot and we saw each other fairly frequently. His senior year was a little hard since we didn't have our weekly outings, but he had really matured with his experiences in the army. Jonathan applied to and was accepted at a state university to pursue aerospace engineering, and he ultimately received scholarships for his academic achievement. His cost after the army helped pay for college was only about $1,000 per semester. He had planned well.

While he was in college we stayed in touch and saw each other on holidays and birthdays. Jonathan joined the university club rugby team and was discovering that college was a great place to be. He was selected by his commander to go to Army Ranger Training and took off a semester to accomplish this very difficult task. Ranger training is widely considered the most rigorous, and those who pass it "the best of the best." Only a small percent graduate and Jonathan was really worried about not being able to meet this challenge.

I happened to be in his city visiting my son the night before he left for the training when he called me on his cell phone, not knowing where I was. I wished him good luck and then drove to his house to give him a hug and tell him personally how proud I was of him.

My "little brother" is now a proud Ranger in the Army National Guard. That timid boy, lacking in self-confidence, has turned into quite an exceptional man. His mom couldn't be prouder.

It's somehow odd that the purpose of organizations like Big Brothers Big Sisters is to find ways for people like me to give something freely to those in need, yet I feel I have learned more from Jonathan than he ever learned from me. He will be my "little brother" forever.

As I write this, Jonathan's unit has been deployed in the latest conflict this world finds itself in; he is in Iraq.

This Thursday I am to bring treats to my daughter's third grade class and am wondering if there are any restrictions as to what I can bring? I want to bring a taco salad since it would be more nutritious than sweets, but the teacher says it is just too messy. I know the custodian in the building and I could call him to see if he agrees. What do you think?

KOLORADO KOOLAID

Can't the Secret Service take a little joke? Good vibrations, man!

One Saturday morning in the early spring of 1973, I got together in the high school band room with four other guys to explore the possibilities of starting a rock and roll band just for the fun of it. Tom was a special education teacher. Bill was an elementary physical education teacher. Kevin was a junior in high school and Danny was a senior in high school.

It was agreed that I would be the drummer and double on trombone, Tom would be the lead singer and promised to learn some musical instruments, Bill would play rhythm guitar and trumpet, Kevin would play bass, and Danny would lead on guitar. In our first session we discovered that while we could play easy songs from the 50s, we were going to have to practice a lot if we were ever going to be a legitimate musical group.

The senior class needed money for their annual party, so they asked our group to play a benefit for them at an elementary school. We agreed. We knew twelve songs and learned five more for that evening. We each made nine dollars and the seniors made about $250, since lots of students came to see three teachers and two students playing together. We had every bit as much fun the seniors did.

The next day we made a promise to each other that we would work hard to make this band a success: we would invest in good sound equipment and better instruments, and we would work to find jobs for the band to play that summer. We needed a name, and Kevin suggested "Kolorado Koolaid." That was the nickname for Coors beer in Colorado, and it became our band's name for the fifteen years that we played music together.

As a result of lots of hard work and many hours of practice, our band developed into a rock and roll show band, and before long we were booked ahead for about a year and a half. We even recorded an album and never had trouble filling nightclubs and lounges with new listeners and a core group of loyal fans.

At length we found ourselves booked into a very popular hotel club lounge. By this time, Danny had dropped out of the group and Jim, an art teacher, had joined as keyboard player. By then we had an entire show that included much more than just playing music: our signature set was a show called "Tommy and the Electratones" where we dressed and acted the parts of different typical characters from the 1950s. We became these "other people" on stage

We dressed as a goody two shoes, a goofball, and a klutz, and each member stayed in character. Tommy's outfit got a lot of attention—he was a body builder and wore tight jeans, a form-fitting white t-shirt, a black leather biker jacket, and dark biker sunglasses; he carried a four-foot shiny chrome tire chain. The t-shirt accentuated his well-defined muscles, so when he took off the jacket, the women in the crowd always went wild.

Our 50s set consisted of a lot of "schtick" mixed in with great music for dancing, but we got a little bit more "schtick" than we bargained for one night with a packed house at the club.

Normally, we performed our 50s set as the third set, changing out of the tuxes we had worn for the earlier sets and into our 50s garb. Our act began after a weekly performance by a famous Dixieland Band from 5:30 until 8:30 p.m. We usually performed at 9:00 p.m., early sets first, then our 50s set. But this Wednesday, the place was packed and the club manager came to our dressing room to ask if we would open with our 50s show so he could hold the larger-than-normal crowd as late as possible. We didn't like the idea at all, but when you work for a club, you do as you are asked.

We got into costume and character, then headed out to the line in front of the club, as we always did, to mingle there and stir things up. Our outrageous and crude, rough behavior scared some of the hopeful patrons waiting to enter. Some regulars knew the routine, but newcomers just stared apprehensively. After annoying a few people, we butted in front of the line and went right on in—causing even more anguish and uproar.

It was all part of the act.

On entering the main room, we spread out and moved toward the stage, stopping by the tables and asking patrons, loudly, if the band was any good. We were loud and rude, saying we'd heard that the band was terrible, that the drinks were watered down, things like that. Tommy, as usual, was slapping his tire chain on some of the tables and braying in his New York accent, "Hey! You! How's it goin'?"

After creating as much havoc as we felt we could get away with, four of us got to the stage—leaving Tommy "terrorizing" more customers—picked up our instruments and launched into the *American Bandstand* theme. Tommy, on cue, started yelling at us from the crowd: "Hey! Whaddaya doin'? Why youse startin' widdout me?" He began pushing and shoving his way among the tables to get to the stage, still yelling and appearing to be very disgruntled indeed.

There were four men seated right in front of the bandstand as Tommy bullied his way toward the stage, all of them wearing expensive three-piece suits. We knew this group had some connection to the Dixieland Band and thought they might be friends or fans, but we had already privately selected them to be the brunt of our "brick schtick," which was coming up shortly. Meanwhile, Tommy had reached their table, and before coming on stage stopped to slam his chain down on it and bellow at them, "Hey! Wha's going on in dis place?"

Imagine our startled surprise when the suited man closest to Tommy reached up suddenly, grabbed him by the jacket collar right under his chin, and pulled him forcefully down to the tabletop so his chin was flat on it. The man said: "Get out of here—this is a classy place and you are causing a disturbance." Poor Tommy was struggling to say, "But I'm part of the show, I'm part of the show!" That's hard to do when you can't move your chin.

To our relief the man quickly let Tommy go and, though very confused, Tommy just smiled at the guys, knowing that they were about to get the surprise of their lives with the "brick schtick." We would get a bigger surprise before it was over.

As usual, Tommy stormed onto the stage while we played the *American Bandstand* theme. It was time for the "brick schtick." Tommy, gesturing and yelling, bent down and picked up one of two bricks on the stage that appeared to be used to weight down some equipment, and threatened loudly to hurt us with it if we didn't stop playing immediately. He made sure the audience saw the brick and heard what he was saying over the microphone. Of course we didn't stop, so he targeted me with the brick and dropped it, just barely missing my foot, but making a very loud thump on the stage. We all quit playing then and reproached Tommy for almost hitting the drummer.

That's when I got up, stormed around the drums, and picked up the other brick. We were the only ones in the room who knew that this second brick was foam rubber. I held it up in a throwing position and said I didn't appreciate what Tommy had done to me one little bit. By now the crowd was yelling and cheering—or squealing. Tommy backed off the stage, begging for forgiveness and mercy and promising never to do that again.

Tommy, of course, backed down right in front of our target table, the "suits" table, and was standing in front of it as I was pumping the "brick" the way a shot putter would hold a heavy shot. The crowd's yelling—and now chanting for me to throw the brick—had risen to a roar. And I hurled the "brick" at him!

Tommy dove out of the way at the last second and the four "suits" bailed out of their seats to the floor, drinks flying as the foam rubber "brick" bounced harmlessly off the table. The audience went nuts. Two of the men at the table had been wearing light-colored summer suits and were drenched from the waist down when they got up. Tommy smiled at them, grabbed a microphone and said, "Enjoy the show—now here's one from the King." And the show went on with a rousing Elvis number as the house employees came rushing, as usual, to replace the drinks of the folks at the "brick schtick victim table," no charge. The place was rocking to the roof!

Our 50s set ended to a wild ovation and we were finally able to take a break and cool off. That's when some of the Dixieland Band people came up and gave us the shock of our lives: they took us to the "suits" table and casually introduced us to four agents of the United States Secret Service. We almost fainted.

What we hadn't been told before was that the Dixieland Band had been invited to play for the President at the White House. The President had made an appearance at the State Fair earlier that day and was doing a fundraiser in the city. While in town, the Secret Service agents were assigned to check out the Dixieland Band prior to allowing them to perform at the White House. The drinks replaced at the end of the "brick schtick" were naturally nothing stronger than iced tea.

The agents were very good sports about the whole thing. They apologized to Tommy for his rough treatment; they thought he was just a troublemaker. They stayed until midnight and bought us drinks on our breaks between our other sets and ended up to be four really great guys.

That should have been all the excitement anyone needed for one night. But it wasn't over for us. The place remained packed until 1:00 a.m. and we were just beat, as we usually were by then. Our last set was supposed to be over by 1:30 a.m., but at 1:15, between songs, Jim leaned over his keyboard and told us that we should play our Beach Boys Medley again. We had already played it earlier in our 60s set, so we looked at him like he had lost his mind! The medley was almost fifteen minutes long, and we rarely played it late at night as it required a lot of high harmony vocals and our voices were pretty tired. Tommy leaned over at Jim and said without the microphone on, "No way—I'm too tired." Jim said softly over his keyboard, "The Beach Boys were the main feature tonight at the State Fair and they just came in and are sitting two tables in front of the stage." Tommy turned around and looked, rolled his eyes toward the ceiling, and away we went into the medley.

After the set, the Beach Boys thanked us for playing the medley for them. We actually sat with them for about ten minutes and visited before they went on to their hotel and we packed up for the night.

On the way home, I couldn't get over all that had taken place in such a short amount of time. I looked at Tommy and said, "Can you believe this evening?" Nobody could say much of anything. To this day it almost seems surreal.

From a senior class fundraiser to Secret Service agents and the Beach Boys, we had just started out as educators having fun in a band and it became much more than we ever imagined. Life is full of possibilities, but no dream is ever realized until it first is dreamed.

Note from an elementary parent:

We were out late trick-or-treating last evening for Halloween and then sat around eating candy until 10:00 p.m. I let Brian sleep in this morning. Please excuse him for being late. Oh, he was dressed like Darth Vadar.